MW01268037

In My Father's Hand

In My Father's HAND

KIARA WESLYN

CROSSBOOKS
PUBLISHING

CrossBooks™
A Division of LifeWay
1663 Liberty Drive
Bloomington, IN 47403
www.crossbooks.com
Phone: 1-866-879-0502

© 2013 Kiara Weslyn. All rights reserved.

No part of this book may be reproduced, stored in a retrieval system, or transmitted by any means without the written permission of the author.

Scripture quotations taken from the Holy Bible, New Living Translation, copyright 1996, 2004. Used by permission of Tyndale House Publishers, Inc., Wheaton, Illinois 60189. All rights reserved.

First published by CrossBooks 08/14/2013

ISBN: 978-1-4627-2815-2 (sc)
ISBN: 978-1-4627-2816-9 (e)

Printed in the United States of America.

This book is printed on acid-free paper.

Any people depicted in stock imagery provided by Thinkstock are models, and such images are being used for illustrative purposes only.

Certain stock imagery © Thinkstock.

Because of the dynamic nature of the Internet, any web addresses or links contained in this book may have changed since publication and may no longer be valid. The views expressed in this work are solely those of the author and do not necessarily reflect the views of the publisher, and the publisher hereby disclaims any responsibility for them.

This book is dedicated to God the Father; His only Son, Jesus; the Holy Spirit; and you, who chose to read this story of God's faithfulness.

"Let them praise the Lord for His great love and for the wonderful things He has done for them. Let them exalt Him publicly before the congregation and before the leaders of the nation" (Psalm 107:31–32). NLT

Special thanks to:

God the Father and His Son, Jesus, who died for me and rose again.

My husband for his love, patience, and faithfulness.

My children for their love, forgiveness, and joy they bring to my life.

My friend, Pebbles, who predicted this book three years before I wrote it.

Jean B., Kim W., Whitney B., Kirsten F., Ms. Dee, Sherri R., Robin W., and Gary R.

Marcus J., Michael B., and Ted F., who did all my technical work for this book.

Brian, Kayla, and CrossBooks Publishing for your patience and for this opportunity.

Contents

Do not be afraid, for I have ransomed you.

I have called you by name; and you are mine.

When you go through deep waters, I will be with you.

When you go through rivers of
difficulty, you will not drown.

When you walk through the fire of oppression,

You will not be burned up; the flames
will not consume you.

For I am the Lord,

Your God,

The Holy One of Israel,

Your Savior.

—Isaiah 43:1–3 NLT

1
His Story through My Story

I've been asked many times in my life, "If you died today, do you know where you would spend eternity?" First John 5:13 always came next: "That you may know that you have eternal life."

I always said, "Yes, I know I would go to heaven," although I didn't really believe it. That answer changed in September 2004.

I was born to alcoholic parents. I am the fourth of five children. I was given to my father's uncle and his wife. I called these people my grandparents. They raised me from the time I was three years old. I grew up in the central United States. I was raised in church. I had good Sunday school teachers and Girls in Action leaders as well as good youth directors. I still remember the songs of my youth and all of my teachers' tireless training. I didn't know it would stick. Proverbs 22:6 says, "Train up a child in the

1

way he should go and when he is old, he will not depart from it." When I was about ten years old, I went down the aisle and said I wanted to be saved. I was baptized. I do not believe that I was saved. I just did it because I thought that would make my grandmother happy.

I was molested by my grandfather. I ran away from home at the age of sixteen. I was put into a home for runaways in 1980. I was put into the juvenile system until a couple from my church gained custody of me. I soon returned to juvenile because I wouldn't behave. I didn't graduate from high school, but I did manage to get a GED. For the next several years, I lived where I could. I had my first child when I was eighteen years old. I moved back in with my grandparents in 1982. My grandmother had a stroke, and I moved home to take care of her until she died in 1985.

I had another child, who my aunt and uncle adopted. I gave him to them when he was two days old. I was sad about this, but I was barely taking care of my first child, and I thought he would be better off with them.

I met my first husband when I was twenty-one. He was older, and I liked that about him. We were married in 1990, and we had three children together. He wasn't very nice to me. I sometimes had to take the kids and live in homes for abused women with children. I lived in constant fear. I became addicted to drugs. I drank all the time. We didn't always have food, and I had to hustle to get food for the kids—but I always had a drink in my hand. I felt that was the only way to handle my life.

Psalm 14:12 says, "There is a path that seems right

unto man but it ends in death." I was living on the path of death and destruction. My life went downhill fast. During all this time, I went to church, but I just didn't think God cared for me. I didn't think I deserved God's love. But I know countless people who went to heaven praying for me. James 5:16 says, "The prayers of a righteous man avails much." Today, I know those prayers saved my life.

I was a stay-at-home mother. I had no education, and I didn't want to work. During this time, the only things I was good at were drinking and doing drugs. Our children were taken away by DHS. Psalm 127:3 says, "Children are a gift from the Lord." I always felt overwhelmed by the needs of my children, which were only basic. I was told to go to AA I was also ordered by the court into anger management. The children were returned, and I stayed sober for almost four years. During this time of sobriety, I did not go to church, but I felt like I should. Proverbs 14:1 says, "A wise woman builds her home but a foolish woman tears it down with her own hands." That is exactly what I did. I constantly destroyed my home by my choices and behavior.

In 1995, I returned to alcohol and drugs. My life went into a downward spiral. I went to jail several times. I hit my children. I cared only for myself, drugs, and alcohol. I couldn't stand to look at myself in the mirror. I knew I needed help. I believed the only way I would ever stop using drugs and alcohol was to die. In 1996, I went to detox and treatment. I was sick. I weighed eighty-nine pounds. I was thirty-two years old. I had nothing to show for my life except hurt children, a loveless marriage, and a drug and alcohol problem.

I moved to another city into a halfway home for women. Here I was introduced to a twelve-step program. I surrendered the fight and realized my life was unmanageable. This program helped me understand my disease of alcohol and drug addiction. This twelve-step program is a program that I am still a faithful member of after sixteen years of sobriety. I attend meetings, and I have a sponsor who helps me when I start thinking only of myself.

When I moved to this new city, God dealt with my heart, and I felt a pull to return to church. I went to a church that was pretty on the outside. I passed it every day as I went to work. It was here that I knew I wasn't saved—that I didn't have Jesus in my heart. Romans 3:23 says, "All have sinned and fall short of the glory of God." Romans 6:23 says, "The wages of sin is death but the gift of God is eternal life through Jesus Christ our Lord." I believed this to be true. I was saved on September 19, 2004. I was baptized.

I went to church faithfully, but then I started hearing things that I didn't believe were true. I quit going to church, thinking that I would find another church. But I didn't. One Sunday of not going to church, and then another, and another—and then I wasn't going to any church or doing anything to build any kind of relationship with God the Father. I thought that was okay. I didn't think God needed me. Philippians 1:6 says, "God who began a good work within you will complete it." I didn't know that God wasn't finished with me.

In this city, I met a man in recovery, and he and I

married in 2000. He is a good man, and I have learned a lot about being in a healthy and loving marriage. We raise my children together and attend twelve-step meetings together. He is very good to me and my children. I am thankful to God to be blessed with such a good husband. I went along thinking, *Now that I am sober, I am much better at everything—a better wife, mom, employee, family member, and citizen. I am doing all right. Now I am succeeding in life!* Isaiah 64:6 says, "We are all infected and impure with sin. When we display our righteous deeds, they are nothing but filthy rags."

One July, my husband and I had a heated argument, and he told me some things about myself that were crushing to my ego and soul. I cried for days and nights. I missed days at work and wouldn't get out of bed. I wanted to die. I wanted to run away from everything. I finally realized that my best was still not good enough. How could it be that after all my hard work I had done to stay sober and make myself a better person, I still did not have it right? How could I be so wrong in all areas of my life? I felt like a complete failure. Second Samuel 22:5–6 says, "The waves of death overwhelmed me: floods of destruction swept over me; the grave wrapped its ropes around me: death laid a trap in my path." I wished for an end. I couldn't go on.

I didn't know what to do. If my hard work all those years didn't bring the peace and joy I needed, then where was I to go, and what was I to do? My husband was worried sick about me. He didn't want to leave me alone. He didn't know what to do. By the grace of God, I didn't kill myself. I was left alone with a loaded gun in the house. I considered using it. I wanted to die, but my pride and ego said, "What will people think?" I thought about my children and all the pain I had caused in their lives. How could I hurt them like that?

I finally realized that I had come to the end of myself. I was broken. My will was smashed. I was nothing and could do nothing on my own. I felt like a dirty rag. I hit my knees and prayed to God to forgive me and receive me back to Him. I realized that I had forsaken my Savior. I forgot how much He loved me. I realized that I had tried to live my life without Him, and I was bankrupt. I realized that I needed Him. First John 1:19 says, "If we confess our sins, He is faithful and just to forgive us our sins and to cleanse us from all unrighteousness." I realized that I had sinned against a holy God. I needed Jesus. I wanted Jesus in my heart and life forever.

I grew up going to a church camp in the summer called Falls Creek. I planned to go to Falls Creek the next week. I still felt depressed, and I thought that running away was the perfect plan. I packed my bags, not really knowing if I was going to Falls Creek or not. I left home and drove. I cried and couldn't seem to forgive myself for being so foolish. I finally ended up at Falls Creek that evening. My heart was still heavy, but I was glad I ended up somewhere safe. That night, at the first service, I was shocked to see the theme of Falls Creek that year: "For Such a Time as This." God spoke to me that night and let me know that He loved me and had prepared the way for me to be at Falls Creek at that time.

Ezekiel 34:16 says, "I will search for my lost ones who strayed away, and I will bring them safely home again." I was overwhelmed! I felt a peace in my heart that I had not felt in a long time, and I knew that God still had a plan and purpose for me. I was willing! I needed to make a public admission. I rededicated my life to Christ that week, and I vowed to find a church to go to when I got home.

On Friday, as I prepared to leave, I saw the camp pastor, Brother J. I told him what had happened to me. He asked me where I lived, and I told him. He asked me about my preference in a church—small or big—and I said, "I'm not going to tell God where to put me. I'll let Him lead me. He knows what I need." He told me about a church. I thanked him. I returned home as a new woman. I had Jesus in my heart. I surrendered to Him.

I visited the church Brother J. recommended in my home city, and I really liked it. I also visited other churches. I kept praying and asking God to lead me where He wanted me to go. After two months, I joined Parkview. My church began ministering to me immediately. I started attending Sunday school and the Wednesday night ladies' group. This church was different! The members cared about me and wanted me to grow to minister to others. I took part in a class that shared the church history and introduced the church staff. I learned what my spiritual gifts are, and I get the chance to use those gifts in the church ministry, I feel a part of a church family. God is making me ready for something great for His glory.

The Monday after I joined the church, the church had

a visiting evangelist named Ken F. God spoke to me the second night. Ken shared his insights on the parable of the seed that fell on the different soil (Luke 8). He explained that the soil represented the different hearts that hear the Word of God. I was stunned to hear that I possessed all those bad hearts! One was hard and cold. One was too crowded. One was counterfeit. One was shallow. I realized that I had given my heart to God but didn't allow Him to change it. I didn't realize that it needed changing. Now I knew why I never matured in Christ. I prayed and asked God to change my heart. I wanted a heart with good soil. God did and is still changing my heart. Ezekiel 36:26 says, "I will give you a new heart and I will put a new spirit in you. I will take out your stony, stubborn heart and give you a tender, responsive heart." He did just that for me.

Today, my relationship with my Father is the most important thing to me. I think about my Savior all day long. I wake early and spend time in the Bible with different Bible meditations. It is my favorite part of the day. I pray and talk with God. He talks to me, and I listen. I talk to Him, and He listens. He has put a song in my heart. I thirst for Him, and I want to honor and please Him in all that I do. I thank Him for keeping me safe and secure and not letting me go.

Romans 8:28 says, "And we know that God causes everything to work together for the good of those who love God and are called according to His purpose." God has forgiven me and come to live in my heart. Jesus paid the price of death for me, and I have the Holy Spirit as my guide. I want others to know what God did in my life. He loves them and will forgive them and come into their hearts too, if they choose. I praise God for loving me and for His complete faithfulness in my life and the lives of those I love. He is still working on His story in me. I can never do enough for Him. I know that Jesus, the Good Shepherd, came and found the lost sheep (me) and carried me home on His shoulders. I was weary from running.

When I get to heaven, I want to see Jesus and say, "Thank you," face-to-face. I want to hug the Savior who died for me. Then I want to see all those who prayed for my life and salvation and say, "Thank you."

Come see and experience for yourself what God can do in your life.

I live because Jesus lives in me.

2
Secrets, Silence, and Loneliness

I was three years old when I went to live at the Nelsons'. My family was at a softball tournament. My dad used to play on a softball team, and we went to a lot of ball tournaments. A man came to our car and was talking to my dad. Then my dad told me to go with Uncle Amos, so I got out of the car and got into Uncle Amos's car. In the car was his wife, Sarah. I went home with them that night. I never went home with my parents again.

Their home was small and nice. I didn't know what to do, so I sat on the couch. Sarah made a place for me to sleep on the couch for the night. It would be my place to sleep for the next ten years.

One time, I woke up crying so loudly that I woke up Sarah. She put me back to sleep. I felt scared and alone. I didn't like the dark when I was at this new home. Soon after I got there, Amos would come to the couch in the

10

night and do things to me in the dark. I didn't really know what was happening to me, but I was scared of him. The next morning, it would all seem like a bad dream. He never said anything to me or looked at me, and Sarah didn't say anything to me either. They never talked to me about anything. They talked to each other but not to me. I lived in a world of silence and secrets.

A family came to visit. I didn't know these people, but they had two little boys, and these boys called Uncle Amos and Aunt Sarah "Grandma" and "Grandpa." I started calling them Grandma and Grandpa too. I never knew my blood grandparents. This worked for me.

My life with Grandma and Grandpa was odd to me. I was a child being raised by an older couple. Our home was clean and quiet. There were no other kids, and there were no pets. I couldn't watch what I wanted on TV. I didn't have a room of my own. No one spoke to me unless I was told to do something. I don't remember being hugged or told that I was loved. When we went to visit people, they were told that my parents didn't want me. I didn't know if that was true, but it made me feel unwanted by my parents. I felt I was lucky that someone was taking care of me, even though the nights were scary.

We went to church a lot. I liked being there. It was fun but mostly, I liked there were children my age there. People were nice to me, talked to me, and told me they were glad to see me. I felt loved there.

I was never a quiet child, and I loved to talk. I would get in trouble a lot for talking too much at home, at church, and at school.

Grandpa Amos was mean and hit me when I got in trouble. He would take off his belt and whip me for something. Many times, I had welts on my back or legs. As I got older, he would slap me in public and yell at me. It always made me feel small and worthless, and I was always embarrassed. Most times, I would cry, but I got in trouble for crying too.

Grandma Sarah was mostly quiet. She was a great cook and could sew very well. She spent her time sewing and cooking. She made me a lot of clothes that I wore to school. I felt different because my clothes were homemade. I didn't have clothes that were in style, and I felt odd. Most times, I dressed like a boy. I grew up as a tomboy. I thought maybe if I looked like a boy, Grandpa Amos wouldn't come to the couch at night.

When I started puberty, I needed a bra. Grandpa Amos and Grandma Sarah's daughter, Joy, bought me my first bra. The start of my menstrual cycle was the most humiliating. No one had ever talked to me about that. What I knew about that was what I had watched at school. The school had shown a film about puberty or something of that nature. That was all I knew. I started one night while I slept. The next morning, I told my grandma, and she was furious that I had ruined her sheets. I had to take those sheets and wash the blood out. It didn't come out, and I was in trouble. This was confusing to me because I felt like I had done something wrong, and I felt dirty. Then I had to go the store to buy Kotex. I was embarrassed because my grandpa took me to the store. I felt humiliated all the time.

My grandparents were very strict, and I didn't have anyone spend the night with me. I wasn't allowed to spend the night anywhere else either. I didn't go to school functions, like football games, and I didn't go to the movies with my friends. I didn't hang out at the pizza place with my friends, and I didn't go to school dances. I didn't have a boyfriend, and I wasn't allowed a car of my own. I did get a driver's permit, but that was only so my grandpa didn't have to drive my grandma around anymore. I didn't ever feel like I was allowed any kind of freedom.

My grandparents told people the bad things I did. I got in trouble a lot at school. I just didn't know how to deal with my childhood or teenage years. I didn't feel like I could tell my grandparents when I didn't understand something in school, and I didn't dare tell them I was having trouble with kids at school. I was criticized, and I felt miserable most of the time at home. I was asked why my grades were so bad, and I just couldn't tell them I didn't understand Math, Science, English, or any subject in school, for that matter.

My world of silence was scary. I was confused most of the time. It seemed I never knew what was going on. One day, I came home from elementary school, and my grandma wasn't there. I asked my grandpa where she was, and he wouldn't say anything to me. I was afraid that we were alone. I didn't want him touching me. But he didn't. He told me to change clothes and that we needed to go. I did as I was told, and we went to the airport. We picked up their daughter, Joy, from the airport. Then we went to a hospital. While I was in the waiting room, I overheard someone say that my grandma had a heart attack, and that was why everyone was at the hospital. That was the kind of silence I lived in every day. I always felt like no one considered me important enough to talk to or explain things to. I never had any idea what was going on.

Once, I got ready for church. I came out of the bedroom to go to church. My grandparents were sitting in the living room. They looked at me, and I realized we weren't going to church because it had snowed heavily the night before. I felt alone and ashamed a lot.

I was athletic, but I didn't join any teams in elementary. I didn't feel I was good enough. I was too afraid to ask for money. I knew I would need money for uniforms, and I was sure my grandparents would say no. Besides, I had to come straight home from school. My only enjoyment after school was *Gilligan's Island*. On one Friday a month, we had movies at school that cost a quarter to watch. I was never given a quarter. I never saw any of the Walt Disney movies until I had children of my own.

I had friends around the neighborhood, and we were all outcasts, but we got along well most of the time. We played as often as we could and spent a lot of time together outside, but sometimes we would come to fistfights, and I gave as good as I got. Sometimes I think I won those fights. I wasn't allowed to go off my street. Even when I got a bicycle, I had to stay on my street. During the summer rains, we stood in my front yard and let the cars splash us with the water that lay in a low spot in front of our house. That was fun.

When I was about twelve or thirteen years old, I saw a little dog running down the street. I called to it, and it kept on running. Later, I saw the dog again and called to it, and it came to me. I gave it some water and some bread. After that, the dog stayed at our house. It was a small, brown-and-white dog; we thought it was half bulldog and half beagle. I named her Pup. She was my buddy, and I liked having her around. She was my friend. We went everywhere together on the block. We ran and played together. She was a small, cute dog.

One day, I noticed that she was getting fat. I chained her to the back of my bike and ran her up and down the road several times. She was running, and she was tired. Her tongue hung out. We went home, and I gave her some water. I didn't know she was having health problems. Soon after that, she was gone. I couldn't find her. I called for her and looked for her on my bike, but I couldn't find her. I was very sad. I missed her and thought she had run away. One time, when I was praying at the dinner table, I started crying for her. I asked God to bring her back. I got in trouble for crying for a dog. I sat in silence and ate my dinner with tears rolling down my cheeks.

I felt ashamed for caring for my dog. About two days later, my dog was back, and she was skinny! She had gone away to have puppies. She was happy to see me, and I was happy to see her! She barked, wagged her tail, and smiled at me. I smiled at her too! I ran outside and gave her a big hug, and she licked my face. We were happy to see each other again. I waited to see where her puppies were. She went into the neighbor's yard under a stack of wood.

After a few days, I brought those puppies home. She had seven puppies. I began the task of keeping track of all those puppies. I was happy. I eventually found homes for all her puppies. Pup was a good mommy. We were together again, Pup and me. People in my family like to bring up that story a lot, especially when I was pregnant with my children. They would say that I was gaining weight and slowing down, and maybe they should strap me to the back of the car and run me up and down the street too. I didn't know my dog was pregnant!

The place I felt loved the most was at church. The church I grew up in was a small. I had friends there. At church, I was allowed to go to some fun things with kids my age, but not everything. I didn't get to go to Jimmy Creek for a week of camping out and Vacation Bible School for the families there. I always wanted to go. I did get to go to Falls Creek most summers if I behaved at school. I tried hard to be good so I could go to Falls Creek.

I used to like the holidays. My grandma was a great cook. She cooked, and we had guests or family. There was fun and laughter in our home during those times.

I wasn't allowed to have boyfriends or phone calls from boys. I don't remember ever having my own radio or TV. I loved to read but didn't have any books I liked to read available to me. I wanted to have a hobby and asked my grandma if I could start a stamp collection. She told me I would have to have money to buy the stamps and that it would be expensive, so I didn't do that either.

We traveled and went on summer vacations. I went to New Mexico, Arizona, Colorado, California, Nebraska,

South Dakota, Arkansas, Kansas, and all the way to Florida during our travels. I liked traveling. I liked to sightsee. My grandparents gave me the joy of traveling.

I wasn't taught to work or to make a living for myself. I didn't have a job in high school, and the one I did get I had to quit because we went out of town. I didn't have any money; however, all my basic needs were met. I thought it was cool that my friends got an allowance.

I didn't have many friends at school. My best friends were at church, and I cherished time with those friends. I did have a lot of girls who wanted to fight me. I didn't know why they didn't like me. I wasn't popular. I didn't date boys. I wasn't smart in class. I wasn't a teacher's pet. I didn't wear the latest fads, but I could fight, and I did a lot of that.

I was good at running. When I was in junior high school, I tried out and made the track and cross-country teams, but I didn't stay on them. I got in trouble for fighting at school, got grounded, and couldn't go to meets. I couldn't run fast, but I could run far. In tenth grade, I went to a cross-country invitational at the Duck Pond on the University of Oklahoma campus. I was excited to go. My coach came to my house and asked for permission for me to go. It was a two-mile run. I placed ninth out of about fifty runners. The first ten runners to cross the finish line received trophies.

I was proud of that trophy and was eager to show my grandparents, but when I showed them my trophy, I was greeted with laughter and jokes that I finished ninth place and still got a trophy. My grandparents didn't understand cross-country. I wasn't congratulated, encouraged, or hugged. Instead, I was laughed at and made fun of. Once again, I was humiliated and discouraged. I didn't run again, and I quit the team. My coach tried to convince me to keep running, but I gave up. I am thankful for that coach, though. She believed in me. I just didn't believe in myself.

By this time, I had moved to the spare room. There wasn't anything in there to let you know this was a teenager's room. My grandpa continued to come to my bed during the night. It still scared me, and I still hated it, but I still didn't say anything about it.

When I was about sixteen years old, my grandparents and I decided that I should be a missionary. I requested to be a sojourner in Tulsa with some friends of ours who attended and pastored at church there. I thought it would be a chance to get away from home for the summer. The closer the time got for me to go, the more I became scared of being away from home. I didn't feel prepared to go and live with people I didn't know, and I wasn't about to tell my grandparents my fears. I felt trapped. I ran away from home.

I hid out and lived with whoever would house me for about a week. I was a runaway, and the police finally found me. I was taken to jail. My grandparents were mad and refused to come get me. I was taken to a home for runaways. I was there for several weeks. A young married couple in my church came to my rescue. They went to court and asked for temporary custody of me, and I lived with them for about six months. Of course, I didn't know how to behave, and I left their home—not by choice. I would like to say that this young couple saved me in more ways than one, and I will always be grateful for them. They stepped up to help a troubled kid, and I will always love and admire them for that. Today, the husband is in heaven, and I stay in contact with the wife.

I stayed away from home for about a year. I stayed with my sister in Florida, making a mess there, when I was put onto a plane and sent back to Oklahoma. My grandmother had a stroke, and my grandfather needed someone to take care of her, so he sent for me. As I went home on the plane, I asked myself, *Aren't these the same people who were so mad at me? I hadn't even spoken to them since I left, and now I am going to help them.* I felt like I had no choice when it came to them. I wasn't even asked if I could come. I was told to do it. I stayed and took care of my grandmother for almost three years until her death.

When my grandmother died, I wanted to leave but had nowhere to go. My grandpa didn't bother me anymore, and by now I had a son. I got in trouble, and my grandpa kicked me out. Family friends kept my son for me because I was living on the streets and staying where ever I could. I told one of my friends what my grandpa did, and she was sympathetic. But one day, I went to visit her, and she started screaming at me and told me that I was lying about my grandpa. I was shocked. My grandpa lied to her and said that I was lying about what he had done to me all those years.

I was down and out. I had nowhere to go. I felt alone, and now, I was mad. I walked to my grandpa's house to tell him what I thought about his lies. He was in the back yard. I grabbed a shovel and was going to hit him with it. He grabbed the shovel, and we wrestled with it. I knocked him down, held the shovel over him, and told him that I was going to knock his lights out. I looked at him and told him, "You molested me since I was three years old. You can deny this to everybody, but you look me in the face, and deny what you did to me!" He couldn't and didn't. Then I told him, "You look me in the eye and admit to me you did what I said you did."

He said, "Okay, I did it!" I could see the fear and the shame on his face. I told him to apologize to me. He did. I threw down the shovel and walked away. The subject never came up again. I realized by that confronting him, I also forgave him. By the time my grandpa died in 2002, I had been in recovery for about six years. I heard that he was sick and in the hospital, and I went to see him. He didn't ever wake up, but I talked to him and let him know I was there. He died a few days later.

When I heard that he died, the first thing I did was sit down and write a good-bye letter to him. In the letter, I thanked him for all the good things that he gave me as I grew up. I thanked him for always giving me a warm bed to sleep in and a hot meal on the table. I thanked him for all the traveling I got to do. I thanked him for taking care of me. I left the letter in the casket with him. My pain over the past was gone, and since I had confronted him face-to-face, the molestation didn't have a hold on my life. I wasn't going to let him have control over my life and mind with his sin. A friend told me if I believe the lies he told me, like I'm not smart enough, then he wins. I will not continue to be his victim.

I lived in world of silence. It seemed that no one explained things to me or talked to me. No one ever seemed to help me to understand what the world was about or anything in it. I learned everything the hard way—but I did learn. The world of secrets I lived in came out after my grandma died. I went into counseling for it. I learned a lot about myself. I learned that if it weren't for my inner fortitude and the love of Jesus, I might not have recovered from the pain in the world of secrets. I lived in a world of loneliness. I was a child growing up in a home of an older couple. I grew up old-school, where the child does not speak unless spoken to. I was raised to stay in the home and depend on the man of the house. I was taught that what happens in the home stays in the home. I was lonely and felt isolated.

But I had a home to call my own. I had food every day. I was clothed. I went to church. I had fun times in my childhood. I did most of my traveling in my childhood. I have fond memories of home too. I don't want to view my childhood in an ugly light. It was just how I was raised. I made all the bad choices in my life on my own. I went down the wrong road by my own choice. I reaped the consequences of my choices heavily.

The grace of God kept me safe on that dark road. The grace of God covered me when I sought Him. I know the words, in Romans 10:13, "whosoever calls on the name of the Lord", will be saved, included me. I know all things can be used for God's glory. I am okay with my life today. My past is used to help other women. My past is for God's glory.

3
The Long Journey Home

In 1996, I was thirty-two years old. I weighed eighty-nine pounds. I had a drug and drinking problem. On September 27, I went to detox at TRC. My husband of seven years went to work, my children went to the fair with their uncle, and I left the home and went to detox. I never went back.

At that time, my children were thirteen, ten, seven, and six. I had given great thought to these children and what would happen to them when I left for recovery. I knew I would leave; I just didn't know when. I thought at one point that I would leave them with relatives, but I didn't know how long I would be gone. I even thought about the Baptist Children's Home but didn't do that either. No choice seemed the right choice. But I had to make a choice, and soon, because I was dying in my addiction, and my children were suffering terribly from neglect.

I decided to leave my children with a relative. I thought that with me gone, my husband at the time, would stop doing drugs long enough for me to get on my feet. I was wrong about that. I didn't realize that the day I left would be a day that would start me on a journey I still travel today. It would be a sad journey for my small children, who were left without a mother and left in the care of someone who was too tied up in his own anger and addiction to ever stop drugs or take care of my children. I left four notes to them about where I was going and why and that I loved them. They never got the notes.

In detox, I realized that I was in severe pain and emotional turmoil. I was prisoner to an addiction that was so powerful that nothing mattered but it. I had lost everything in my life to my addiction. I sat alone, confused, angry, and ashamed. I finished a seven-day detox program and waited for an opening for treatment. I realized that seven days were not enough for me. I needed more help. A treatment facility opened up for me called New Hope. I went and stayed for thirty days, and I learned a lot about myself and my disease. One week, I had to look at the damage I caused my family. My heart broke, and I cried many days and nights over my children. I loved them very much, but I never knew how to show it. I was always angry and overwhelmed. I was a kid when I started having kids, so I failed miserably in every way as a parent.

After treatment, I knew I needed more help. I waited for an opening at a halfway house for women. Halfway to where? I often wondered. An opening came at a halfway house called 12 and 12. During the times I waited to get in anywhere, I hid at my friend's home. My husband at the time, was looking for me. No one gave me away, and I had my friend and aunt look in on my kids while I was away.

My friend drove me to 12 and 12. She told me the same thing she told me at treatment: "Don't call me, 'cause I'm not coming to get you." I was scared and alone, but not as scared and alone as I felt when I was using drugs and drinking. I stayed there for seven months. I met a guy from Texas who was there for the same thing, recovery, and we became friends. We cared about each other, but not seriously. I let him know that I was getting out of a bad marriage, and I wasn't looking for another one. I let him know that I had children I had left in search of sobriety, and someday, they were going to come back to me. I was going to get my children, and if he didn't want a family, then he should not seek after me. I knew what I wanted, and nothing was going to stand in my way. I had no idea that the journey to get those kids back would test the very faith I built my hope on and my newfound sobriety in ways I couldn't imagine.

My boyfriend and I moved out of 12 and 12 together, and I immediately started looking for my kids. I looked for my oldest son first because I knew where he would be. I found him running around in the city. He was shocked to see me, and I could tell that he was angry at me. He didn't like me showing up after nine months and bringing a guy with me. It took a lot of talking and convincing to get him to come live with me. I think he wanted to see what was going on and if I was really sober. He moved back with me just in time for me to put him in school. We lived in a two-bedroom apartment and started learning how to live with each other as healthily as we could.

During this time, I had a chance to make amends to my son for all the things I put him through as he was growing up. I was mean to him and used to hit him. I used to slap him, yell at him, and make him take care of his younger brothers and sister when he was just a child himself. He lived in fear of me and never knew what I was going to do when I started drinking and doing drugs or where I would leave them. I often left them alone at home and made my oldest son take care of them until I got home. Sometimes it would be all night and all day until I came back. I made him change diapers, help potty train his younger brother, and wash out dirty cloth diapers. I found out later that he flushed those down the toilet.

I always cussed and screamed at my son. I never encouraged him. I didn't say I loved him much; somehow, I figured he knew that already. I just never knew how to show it! No wonder my children hated me; I hated myself and had no respect for them or myself. I tell people that my children and I grew up together. My son's only saving grace during this time was his grandpa. He lived in the same neighborhood we did, and my son knew he could always go there and stay. He often stayed there to get away from me and all that darn responsibility he was forced to take on by his drunk, drug-addicted mom. Once, I was so wired up on drugs that I became paranoid, and my son had to drive me home. He was thirteen years old. He had to do that more than once.

I tried to do right by my son now that I was sober. I provided a decent home for him and let him know that I loved him. I told him I loved him every day. He went to a lot of twelve-step meetings with me. He slowly learned about my recovery and all that I was trying to do. He forgave me. What a gift. He had a lot of troubles to work out in his own life, but he knew that I was changing and that I was there for him. He knew I was dedicated to sobriety and that I was serious about not drinking or doing drugs anymore. I believe that was a gift to him, and I truly believe that he needed that. I also made living amends to him and spent time with him.

We had a day after work when we did whatever my son wanted. I tried to let him know that he was important to me, just like everything else in my life, and set time aside just for him. We had a lot of fun together, and I enjoyed getting to know my son. I found out that he is super funny and has a great way of laughing at the past. That helped me to get over the past too. He is smart and knows fortitude and strength unlike anything I ever encountered in a man as young as he was. It has been a great joy to watch this son grow up, have children of his own, and be a great dad. He is patient and kind and holds and hugs his sons. He tells them he loves them and never yells at them. He teases them a lot and smiles at them often. He plays with them and teaches them with much patience. It pains me to know that I could have done that with him, and he would have understood the same. I just didn't know how.

My husband at the time realized that I wasn't coming

back. He called me at 12 and 12 to tell me that the kids needed me. He told me that he needed me. We both realized I wasn't coming back. He left with the kids. I didn't know where they went.

When my son came to live with me, we decided to start to find the kids. I had been sober about a year. My son and I started by going to the last school they were at to see if there was a transfer to another school. We went to where they were transferred, and they had been removed from school without a forwarding address. We went by the house where my husband at the time, mother had last lived, and the house was deserted. The school told us about where the kids lived, and we went there. A neighbor came out and told us that they had just moved out about a month ago. We were tired and went home.

I went to court in 1998 to ask for a legal divorce from the ex and was granted the divorce and full custody of the kids, even though I didn't know where they were for almost four years.

During this time, I stayed sober, but I cried all the time about the kids, and I missed them terribly. Where were they? Were they together? Were they all right? Who were they with? Did they miss me? These questions and more haunted and controlled me. My sponsor kept telling me to stay sober so when they came back to me, I would know how to live sober with them. She always encouraged me and kept telling me they would come back. I didn't really believe her, but I did what she said. Most importantly, I didn't do what she told me not to do.

Once in 1998, my son and I were in the city, looking

for the kids, and we saw them at the neighborhood laundromat. When they saw me, they were shocked, scared, and confused. I was the same way. I didn't know what to do. I wanted to grab them and run, but I had been instructed by my attorney if I ever saw them to find out where they were living and get them legally with the police. It was hard for me to drive away and leave them there. We found out where they were living, and we headed back home to tell my attorney. By the time we got everything in place, they were gone again. I was sick at heart. They were in my arms, and I let them go again. I felt deep regret. I let my sponsor and attorney know my frustration. Again, I leaned on my sponsor for support. She was with me during some of my lowest mama moments.

I tried over the next years to find my children, but it seemed they had gone to another state. They had family in other states, but I didn't know how to find them. Without God, my sponsor, my boyfriend, and the twelve steps, I would have lost my mind. I didn't know it at the time, but God was working something out for His glory.

My son started having problems in all areas of his life, and so did my boyfriend and I, so I sent my son back to his grandpa, and my boyfriend and I separated. For a year, I came to term with my life and did some personal reflection. I still made trips to the city. During one visit to the city, my son told me the kids' uncle had died and that they were back in the state. He told me that my daughter and youngest son were living in Arizona, but the uncle died, and they were back. He said that his younger brother was with his grandma somewhere.

My boyfriend and I got back together, and in 2000, we got married. When we finally got right in God's eyes, I started having dreams of the kids. In the first dream, I could see the kids, but I couldn't touch them. I was talking to them, but it seemed they couldn't hear me. In the next dream, a week later, I could see my youngest son in an attic. He was beat up, bruised, and crying. In the next dream, a week later, I went to their house and checked it out. It was small and narrow. In the next dream, a week later, I dreamed their father called me and said, "If you want the kids, come get them right now." I woke up and knew in my heart that something was about to happen.

One day at work, a lady walked in and asked me, "Are you Kiara?" I told her I was, and she handed me something and left the store. I opened up a letter that said I was to appear in court to dispute the custody matter of the kids by their father. I was stunned. I went to my attorney, and he said, "Good. Now we will know where the kids are." He assured me that this was a good thing. I wasn't so sure. I would have to face the ex in court, and I hadn't seen him in several years. I was afraid, and I wasn't sure why.

The long journey home for the kids began. It would test me, try me, and cause me to cry out to God for help more than once. We went to court. I saw the ex but no kids. In court that day, the judge ordered the ex to return the kids to my husband and me. This was the same judge who had given me the kids in my divorce. We needed a court order from the judge, and my attorney needed to print that up, so we left the court and rushed to his office.

We were supposed to meet my ex and the kids in the town where they lived. We went to the police station in that town with the order from the judge. We were supposed to meet a 5:00 p.m. We waited, but they did not show. We went with the police, who knew the address, but there was no one there. Neighbors said the family had packed up and moved hastily that afternoon. I had a court order and no kids. We returned home, and I was sick, angry, and frustrated. My attorney filed a motion, and another court date was set.

The court date arrived, and there were no kids, but now they had an attorney for the kids. She said the kids didn't want to see me or live with me and that she feared for their safety if they came with me. I was steaming and prayed to keep my mouth shut. Another court date was set, and this time, my ex was ordered to bring the kids to court. I was furious. He looked at me. I smiled back.

The court date came, and the kids were there. They were in a room with a window, and I could see them but not talk to them. They could see me too. I remembered the dream. In the first dream I had, I could see the kids, but I couldn't touch them. Another court date was set. The next time, I would be able to talk to them. We were assigned a guardian *ad litem*. She was supposed to look out for the interest of the kids. Again, I had full custody of the kids and no kids. I was frustrated and angry with the whole ordeal. The kids' attorney said the kids were afraid of me and that they needed to get to know me before I could be alone with them. I was court-ordered into parenting classes and was told that when those were completed, I could possibly have visitation rights. What? Visitation rights? I had full custody, and I would get visitation rights? I was angry, but I kept smiling. Another court date was set—about three months into the ordeal.

By the next court date, my husband and I had taken the parenting classes and sent the judge personal references from our friends and colleagues. Our first set of visitation dates was set. We went to the town where the kids lived. I walked into the house and remembered the second dream. I went to see where the kids lived. We took the kids and made note of the living arrangements. The kids seemed to like the visits with us. They were excited to see where and how we lived. My children seemed to handle the stress of the custody battle well and rarely spoke of their home life, although, they did enjoy making fun of the girlfriend. They seemed to get along well.

My husband and I took the kids to a lot of 12 step meetings and spent a lot of time with them. The visits were short, and the time it took to travel from our home to their house on Friday and back again on Sunday night took a toll on us. At the next court date, we asked that the ex- and girlfriend bring the kids to us. they agreed to bring them halfway. This went on for several weeks. I was very tired. My patience was wearing thin, and I had a hard time keeping it together.

During one visit, I went to meet the kids at the pick-up point, and I noticed that my youngest son had a large bruise on his cheek. I remembered the third dream in which Jodie was beat up, and I asked him what happened to his face. He told me some ridiculous story. I was angry, and I couldn't get him to tell me the truth. He finally told me what happened, and it was no accident. Someone had grabbed Jodie's face and squeezed it so hard that it left a bruise in his cheek. The more comfortable the kids became with us, the more the truth started coming out about their life without me. It was sad, and I was angered to hear it.

We found out that after I left for detox, the kids were living with different people. They moved around constantly, staying with different people. Finally, they ended up with the grandma, but my two youngest children went to live with family in Arizona. They told me of their life there, and it was heartbreaking. Family members had died suddenly, and they had to move back with their dad. I was shocked at the many things that kept me from finding the kids.

During this time in court, I realized that my children were being left in the custody of someone they weren't related to. I told this to my attorney, and we tried another approach, using the Indian blood of the kids and the tribal courts. My children were on all kinds of needless medicine for things that could have been controlled by proper parenting and love. Every time the kids came to visit, I threw all the medicine in the trash. They told me they missed a lot of school. I asked them about their grades and study habits. They didn't have to go to school if they didn't feel good. I sent a copy of the court papers to the school and requested their school transcripts and attendance records. I then sent a copy of these records, which were terrible, to the district attorney; claimed truancy; and requested a reason for this from their dad. The tribal courts agreed with our claim and started filing the needed paperwork to bring the case to the tribal courts to settle.

The tides were turning, and we stared to tighten the screws. My children told me their dad and his girlfriend received a court summons to appear in juvenile court to answer the claims of truancy. They were both very upset. One of my kids was hospitalized for stress in this matter. He had stomach problems that his doctor said was caused by him having to see me in court. My attorney looked to find where this doctor went to school and where she did her residency, and he couldn't find any information on her in any of the fifty states of America. We ordered her to court as well.

One day, as my husband and I ate breakfast, a man approached the house. I was served a summons to appear in court for a protective order filed against me by the girlfriend. I couldn't believe it. I went to court and the girlfriend never showed up. My children told me later that they told the girlfriend how I kicked-boxed and how I used to fight a lot. She became afraid of me.

One weekend, I drove to the pick-up point to get the kids for our visit, and the girlfriend didn't bring them. I waited for an hour and a half. I was furious and afraid that they ran off with the kids again. I called my attorney.

While driving back home, I had a heart-to-heart with God. I was tired of playing this game. I was frustrated. I was afraid, and my heart was weary and heavy. I couldn't do it anymore. My fight was gone. I was done. I said, "God, if I'm not going to ever get those kids back, please give me the courage and strength to go on with my life without them. But if I am supposed to get them back, do it now. I'm done!" It had been a grueling six months, and I was tired of jumping through hoops. I wasn't going to do this anymore. I went home and cried for a couple of days.

One morning—I think it was a Saturday—I got a call from the children's father. He told me if I wanted the kids, I should come get them right away. I called my attorney. My husband, my attorney, and I went to move the kids to my home. As we drove, I remembered the last dream, in which I got a call from their father and went and got the kids. It had all happened just like my dreams had indicated it would happen. I know today God was letting me know I would get the kids back. My heart soared, and I praised God.

I would like to tell you that everything was fine and dandy after the long journey home, but that is not the case. My children were in a world of hurt and confusion. They had a bone to pick with me, and I had a lot of questions to answer. Through the grace of God and the power of the twelve steps, I was able to answer those questions and quiet the fears and doubts in all of my children. Today, we are strong and united. We've gone through hard times together, but God has allowed us all to be together again, and we are thankful to God for that precious gift.

4

His Daddy

During the summer I was eighteen years old, I lived with my mother. I was a credit short of graduating high school and attending a summer school. My sister came home from Florida to visit. My sister was ten years older than I was and had left home at eighteen. She had been married for at least ten years by this time. Her husband was in the air force and was stationed at Eglin AFB in Florida. They had four small children.

After turning eighteen, I felt like I needed to be allowed to do whatever I wanted. I was all grown up, and no one was going to tell me what to do anymore! I had a friend whose boyfriend sold drugs, and she and I became great friends. My mother was always mad at me because I always did just what I wanted. I was always in some kind of trouble and didn't hang out with the best people, but that was okay with me because I wasn't the best either. I liked to drink and stay out. I had another sister who lived at home. We did a lot of things together, but she knew I had a lot of problems.

My sister came down in late June from Florida, and was going home in July. She asked me to go back with her. I think she wanted to get me away from my friends. I asked her husband if it was okay for me to go back with them, and he said yes. I left with them and their four kids in a car for a three-day trip back to Florida.

My sister had a good life and a good home. Her whole life centered on her children and home. She was a great wife and mom. I liked spending time with her and her family.

My brother-in-law played on the base softball team, and I went to games with him and my sister. I liked the military guys and thought they were handsome. They guys on the team liked my brother-in-law and sister, and I was introduced to their friends. They introduced me to Mitch. He was tall, lean, and handsome, had a great athletic body, and had a great smile and blue eyes. I liked him a lot. I only saw him at the games. One day, after the game, he asked my brother-in-law if he could take me out. He said yes, and so did I.

Mitch took me out to eat. I noticed when he paid the bill with a check that he went by his middle name. We went to the movies. He took me to the beach. Sometimes we just talked. He told me that the opening scene in the movie *The Night the Lights Went Out in Georgia* was filmed in his hometown in Tennessee. One night, he took me to the barracks. I was pretty ignorant to military things, but I realized that he lived there. He took me to his room. I noticed a picture by his bed. It was of a little boy and girl. They were cute, but I didn't ask about them. We fooled around that night. I thought this guy was nice and that he liked me. We talked, and he took me home.

I liked this guy, and I told my sister about Mitch. She told me this guy was married and had kids. I realized that the kids in the pictures were his children. I didn't want to be in the middle of a marriage. I knew then that he was using me, and my sister didn't want me to see him anymore. I didn't want to see him anymore either. I started dating other guys. By late August, I started to get on my sister's bad side. I just did what I pleased, drank all the time, and stayed out.

One day, I came home, and my sister told me to get my stuff together; I was going back to my grandparents' home. My grandmother had a stroke, and my grandfather sent for me to come home. He paid for a plane ticket. I was very worried and flew home immediately.

I left Florida in a mess, just like I left everywhere else. I had wrecked the car of my sister's friend's son. I charged up a high phone bill talking to a guy at another base and did the same thing with the home phone of one of her friends. My sister was furious with me. I was afraid to talk to her. She wanted me to pay for the damage but knew I couldn't. She told me not to call her again and said, "Thanks a lot." I felt bad, but that was what I always did to people. I cared only for myself and what I wanted. I had a drug and drinking problem. I didn't know how to change. I was only eighteen and didn't know anything about life. I didn't care to know. Little did I know that my life was about to change forever.

I stayed and took care of my grandmother. She was paralyzed on one side and couldn't take care of herself anymore. I slept on a cot in her room so I could help her get up to go to the bathroom or get her something to drink. I noticed that I was gaining weight and wasn't getting my regular cycle each month. I realized that I was pregnant!

Fear gripped me. I had to think of what to do. I was eighteen and unmarried. I knew the father was Mitch. I didn't know what to do. My sister didn't take my calls, and I didn't know how to get a hold of him either. I was afraid and alone. I couldn't talk to my grandparents about it. I could never talk to them. I was alone and ashamed. I was afraid to be happy that I had a life growing inside of me and that I would be a mommy. I always wanted to be a mommy. I was afraid of what people would say about me. I grew up very religious, and unmarried girls didn't get pregnant. I tried to hide my stomach. I was small in my youth, so it didn't take long for everyone to find out. A nice lady from my church asked me if I had started seeing a doctor yet. I said no. She advised me that I should. My grandparents already knew; they just hadn't said anything yet. When my grandmother did say something, I felt ashamed. I wanted to cry or die. Thank God for one of my aunts.

My aunt helped me a lot. She talked to my about being pregnant and help me not feel so bad. She helped me laugh and enjoy my first pregnancy. No one ever asked me who the father was. I think everyone knew I got pregnant in Florida.

B. was born May 2, 1983. He was the light of my life. He was cute and smart. My aunt saved both of us during that time. She came and took him from the hospital to her house. My grandfather said, "That baby is not allowed in my house." I felt angry and sad. He wanted me to give up my baby, but I wouldn't do it. He was mad and thought if the baby wasn't allowed at the house that I would just give in to his demands. He was wrong. I stayed at my aunt's house. She had to teach me everything about a baby—I mean everything. I had never been around kids and didn't know how to be a mommy, especially to a newborn. My aunt was patient and showed me what to do and what not to do. I was happy to be B's mommy and loved him very much. I was sad in my heart because I knew he would grow up not knowing his father. I carried this pain and burden in my heart for twenty-seven years.

In 2010, I was forty-six years old and in a different season of life. I faced aging, wrinkles, and pains in my body for no apparent reason. For the past fourteen years, I had looked back and tried to repair the mistakes of the past. One of my greatest regrets was that my oldest son, who was twenty-seven, still didn't know who his father was, where he was, or if he was even alive. I carried the pain of uncertainty, and so did my son, who was also a father with two sons of his own. God began to stir my heart, and the Spirit began to move me.

I watched *Troy, the Locator* on TV one night. I was moved by the reunions of children with lost parents. I got on the computer and logged on to his website. There were questions, such as "Who are you looking for, and why?" I answered them, left a contact number, and went to work. About two days later, my phone rang. A lady from the show wanted to talk about my search. We talked for a while. She was gathering information. She asked the questions, and I cried when I answered. I felt ashamed that I didn't know much about the man who fathered my child. I only knew three things about him—that he was at Eglin AFB in the summer of 1982 and played ball on the base softball team, his name and the fact that he went by his middle name, and that the opening scene of the movie *The Night the Lights Went Out in Georgia* was filmed in his hometown in Tennessee. That was it. She was comforting and let me know they could probably find him, but it would cost $700. I said okay. She said she would send me the application, and I told her I would send the money.

I talked with my husband later that evening. He said that we didn't have that kind of money and could find him for less than that. I said, "Okay, find him!" My husband has a family member with access to high level security people, and we talked to them. Next, we talked to my husband's friend, who had a high level of access in computers. Next, we talked to a bounty hunter we knew. Then I remembered a friend who worked for a private investigation company.

At that point, I was overwhelmed by telling so many people the story of my search, and my heart was heavy. My friend referred me to someone in her office. I spoke with Dane. I told him what I knew about B's dad. He told me that his last name was common, even in the military, and it might take him some time to look around. He didn't sound encouraging, but I was hopeful. I asked him how much the search would cost, and he told me not to worry about it. He rounded off a number—less than $700. He said not to pay him yet and give him some time. He took my number, and we left it at that. It was a Tuesday.

The following weekend, I misplaced my phone. I found it on Tuesday. I noticed I had messages and listened to them. Dane had called and wanted to talk in his office. I was getting ready for work. I called in and let my workplace know I would be late. I went to see Dane. He was nice and greeted me. I sat down at his desk. He told me he found a guy with the same name, and he was stationed at Eglin in 1982, but he wasn't sure when in 1982 he was there. There was a whole file, and he said there were an e-mail address and a picture. My stomach was in knots, and my heart beat fast. I felt flush. I paid him, and he handed over the file.

I didn't look at the file until I got home. My husband was there, and he waited for me to look at it. I first looked at the picture. It was an older guy. He didn't look familiar to me. He was smiling, and there was an attractive woman with him. I kept looking at the guy. I couldn't tell if it was him or not. I hoped it was. I know time changes people, and I couldn't be sure. My husband asked me if it looked like him. I didn't know. I felt many emotions. I wanted to cry, but I didn't know why. I hoped it was him. I looked over the information. I saw the e-mail address. I didn't know what to do.

I decided to see if the man in the file was B's father. I got on the computer and sent him an e-mail. I asked him if he was at Eglin AFB in the summer of 1982 and if he played on the base softball team. I sent it and went to work. On my first break, I checked, and he had responded. He told me he was there, and he did play on the team. He asked a question about my brother-in-law. I responded. I asked if he remembered a pretty little Indian girl who visited that summer. I told him I wasn't there long. I told him that I used to come to the games with my brother-in-law and asked if he remembered me. I sent my response and went back to work.

At lunch, I checked, and he had responded. Yes, he remembered me! He asked me how in the world I ever found him. I was happy and overwhelmed! *What now?* I was a basket case. I was out of my mind, and my coworkers wondered what was going on with me. I knew it was him, and he remembered me. I didn't know if I would ever be able to speak to him again. I told him the truth. I told him I paid a private investigator to find him and why—we had a son together. I told him his son's name and said that his son was twenty-seven now and a father himself. They had the right to know each other. I apologized for telling him in this way. I told him it was for B that I made the search for him, Mitch. I told him it was my fault they didn't know each other and asked what he wanted to do next. I sent the message and went back to work.

On my way to my car after work, I started bawling. I was crying so hard that I couldn't walk or drive. I just sat in my car and cried for a long time. I didn't know why. I waited and checked my e-mail at home. I kept communicating with Mitch to calm him down. I knew he must have been out of his mind too. I apologized for running over him with that Mac truck and for just now telling him. I explained that I was young and didn't know what to do because he was married then. I told him we didn't want money and that my intent was not to harm him or mess up his life. He had the right to know. I just wanted him to get to know B. They both deserved to know each other. I apologized and waited.

About three days later, B's father responded. He said he wasn't trying to ignore me, but his life was flipped upside down, as well as those of his family members. He couldn't understand why he was just now finding this out. I told him it was my fault. He said he had his own questions too. He asked B's last name and birth date and whether B knew that, he, Mitch didn't know about any of this. He also said that he believed everyone should know who their father is and wanted that for B. He asked B to contact him if B wanted to.

I was relieved and sent a response back. First, I wanted B's dad to know that any questions he or anyone else had must be answered by me. I didn't want my son to answer questions that were not his to answer. I told him I wasn't afraid and could take the heat. I told him not to feel guilty about this and not to come into a relationship with B like that. B would know and feel like his dad was only doing this because he felt like he had to, and that wouldn't be good. I told him to just get to know his son. I also told him that I would have to tell B that I had found his father.

B would contact him; I just didn't know when. I thanked him, but really, no words could express how thankful I was for B. I respected Mitch, B's father, for listening to me, believing me, and taking the time to reach out to B.

I told B when he was younger that I would try to find his dad for him. I didn't know how or where to start. I didn't know much about him or whether he would remember me. Twenty-seven years had gone by. I didn't have the courage or means to find Mitch. But things were different now, and I found him with God's help. I wondered when to tell B.

On Sunday, I went to church. I had prayed for B and his father to meet for years. I was so thankful to God for allowing this to happen. I was afraid of how my son would take this news. I called him after I came home from church that day and told him to come over alone. I needed to talk with him. He sounded hesitant and asked if I was okay; I said yes. He showed up about thirty minutes later. I met him in the dining room.

I had papers on the table about B's father. I started to cry. I knew my son was scared, and so was I. Finally, I said, "Remember a long time ago, I told you that I would find your father for you?"

B said, "Yeah."

I said, "Well, I found him." I handed him the folder about his dad and said there was a picture of him. B was very quiet. He didn't say anything but had a look on his face that I didn't understand. Finally, he said, "Mom, you told me years ago that you saw my dad somewhere and told him you were pregnant with me, and he said he didn't care." I was stunned. I didn't remember saying that to him. I told him it was untrue. I don't know why I said that. His father didn't know about him, and that was my fault. I probably said that to cover my own guilt while I was drinking or stoned. I told him I was sorry and that I found his dad. Mitch said it was okay for B to contact him if he wanted to.

B had another look on his face I didn't understand. I asked him, "What is the matter?"

B got up, got a glass, and poured a drink of water. He asked, "What am I supposed to tell my brothers and sister?"

I asked, "About what?"

B asked, "About finding my dad? Don't you think it will make them feel bad because of their dads?"

I was stunned again, and I wanted to cry. The heart of my son, who just found out who his father was, was concerned about how his siblings would feel about that. I said, "No, B. They know who their fathers are, but you are the one who didn't know. Now you do. They will be happy for you."

B sat down again. There was silence between us. Finally, he said, "Mom, I have to go." As he got up to go, he took the file with his daddy's information, and hugged me. Before he walked out, he stopped and said, "Thanks. I guess." Then he left.

I was relieved to get through that, but I was somewhat taken back. I thought B would have a different reaction. I was left with questions of my own. B didn't ask any questions and didn't say anything. He didn't even look at the picture of his dad. I thought the "Thanks" would be bigger. I called my aunt. We talked, and I told her what happened. She said that maybe B was dealing with the fact that I lied to him about his dad. Maybe he thought all these years that his dad had rejected him. He was dealing with both of those untruths right now. She told me not to worry and that B would talk to me about it later. She told me to give him some time. She reminded me that the two of us went through a lot of things together, and we would get through this too. She said my son loved me, and he would come around.

I texted B about an hour later and asked if he had told anyone about his dad. He told me he told his wife and brother. I was excited to know what they thought, but B told me, "Mom, I've had a very emotional day. My friend got in a bad car accident, and now this. I don't want to talk about it." I didn't respond. My feelings were hurt, and I was confused. I was having a *very* emotional time as well. Making the decision to find Mitch wasn't easy. Then, when I found him, it wasn't easy telling B's father about a son he didn't know he had. I had to reassure him it was okay, and then I had to turn around and tell my son that I found his dad. I was *very* emotional. I was happy that I found Mitch, but I was worried about how my son was taking the news. I thought about my other children and the future. I talked with my husband. I felt a little sorry for B's dad. I knew he was having a hard time too. My husband was unsympathetic. He said, "That's what he gets for taking advantage of my sweetie." I laughed. It made me smile.

On Monday, I went out of town for a week. B tried to call me and texted me often, but I didn't respond. I didn't talk to him for several weeks. I was still hurt and didn't know what to say to him. Finally, he asked me what was wrong, and I told him I was trying to leave everyone alone. I was tired of trying to do the right thing and someone getting mad at me. Then B told me that he had contacted his dad through e-mail. He did this the day after we talked. B's dad was nice enough. Mostly, B was glad his dad wasn't being difficult about anything. Mitch sent B some pictures, and B got to see what his father looked like. Mitch told B that he was married for more than twenty years and had two daughters. One of them had a name that starts with a *B*. B liked that.

B and his father talked a lot through e-mail. My friend make a CD with a timeline of pictures of B from the time he was a week old to the present and sent it to Mitch so he could see his son grow up in pictures. We also found out that B's youngest son and Mitch had the same birthday. Things looked like destiny for them.

B started asking his dad some hard questions. B asked about the marriage that Mitch was in when he and I met. B found out that he had an older brother and sister by his father's first marriage. B has a large family of siblings. He has an older brother, an older sister, and two younger sisters from his father's side and three younger brothers and a younger sister from my side of the family. The younger sister he grew up with wasn't happy to learn that she wasn't the only sister anymore, but was graceful and loving to her older brother.

B is healthy and happy today. He is a husband and father. He is a good son. He has lived through good and bad times in the quietness of his heart. He is a good person. B didn't have a pleasant or super happy childhood, and it is a testament to his own character that he has achieved all that he has today. He has fortitude and courage. A whole new chapter of his life began, and I know in my heart that it will continue in peace and happiness. I am happy and grateful to God for allowing us all to come back together. I am grateful that God put back together what I broke.

I spoke with my Christian friend at work about being overwhelmed with tears when I left work the day I found B's dad. She said, "That's what happens when God relieves our burdens. When we get tired of carrying them, and He takes them, that was relief you were feeling." I almost started crying again! I hadn't realized how heavy the burden in my heart was until I let it go and gave it to God. I am very thankful to God for His mercy and grace in my life and the lives of those I love.

B apologized to me for becoming distant after I found his dad. He was just trying to deal with everything and didn't know what to do. He told me that when he deals with things, he wants to be alone. I realized that I do the same thing. He told me he would always keep me informed of his relationship with his dad. I am happy about that.

Mitch told B that they would meet in 2011. I knew it would be good and make B happy. I know this meeting is by God's divine appointment!

B finally met his daddy. It was a good visit, and B returned happy. It was a weekend visit with just the two of them. B got to meet his father's wife, and she was nice to him as well. B plans to meet everyone in his father's family. He enjoys talking with his siblings on Facebook.

I am very thankful to God for His perfect timing. I am thankful that He repaired what I broke and allowed us to all come together when all of us were ready. Praise the Lord, my soul!

I am also thankful to Mitch for taking the time to get to know his son. I know it wasn't an easy thing to do, and I admire the strength he has. In kindness, he allowed B to come into his life and be a part of his family.

It has been an incredible journey for us, and I give God all the glory!

5
And Then He Came Home

Gabriel is my second child and my second-born son. He is funny, handsome, and likes to play basketball. He gets along well with his brothers and sister. You couldn't tell by looking from the outside that these children weren't raised together. Gabriel came back into our family in 2004.

The year was probably 1980. It was the summer, and my grandparents and I were preparing to go the annual picnic at the Moore family home. It was always fun to go, and we stayed all day. We ate good food, watched TV, and visited with everyone there. Sometimes, we popped fireworks. Sometimes, the kids played games—volleyball, softball, or Frisbee. We were always outside. What made this day so much fun was that I got to see Willis. He was there with his family, and I thought he was handsome. We were always competitive, so I didn't think he noticed me or even cared that I was there. I was more like friendly competition. I found out later that he did notice me, and he did care.

I visited my aunt on the weekends. I was about fifteen years old, and lived with my grandparent who were very strict. My aunt came to get me on the weekends so I could have some fun. We went to garage sales, watched movies, or played games and just had good times. What my grandparents didn't know was that my aunt let me see Willis when I came to visit on the weekends. He lived around the corner from my aunt. He came over, and we sat outside or just hung out together. Sometimes we went on dates, out to eat, to a movie, or sometimes to parties that his friends had. Most the time, we just hung out at my aunt's house. We knew that we really liked each other, but we weren't boyfriend and girlfriend. I only got to see him on the weekends, and it wasn't every weekend.

He and I dated during our high school years and stayed close, even though I was raised by my grandparents, who were strict. When I was sixteen, I left home and was put into the custody of a young couple from my church. During this time, I got to see him on a regular basis. We had lots of fun.

He went into the army, and we lost touch. He found me somehow and gave me a ring that was supposed to be an engagement ring. We lost each other again and by now, I had my oldest son. Willis came home from the army, we started seeing each other again, and I got pregnant. It was the summer of 1984. My grandpa kicked me out of the house, and I had nowhere to go, so I moved in with him and his parents. We tried to do the right thing. We talked of marriage and started making plans for a wedding. His parents thought it was the right thing to do, but something happened, and he became distant from me. He didn't want to talk or get married. I couldn't figure out what was going on. Eventually, I moved out and on with my life. But I was pregnant, alone, and back at home with my grandpa because I had nowhere to go. What would I do?

I was close to my aunt, and I told her that I couldn't have this baby and was considering an abortion. I felt like I had no choice, but she said not to do that. She reminded me that her sister had been married for at least ten years and had tried to have a child but couldn't. I could give my baby to them to raise. I didn't know what to do. Could I do that? Could I adopt my child out? I considered the thought. I tried to make contact with Willis to see what he thought, but he was not interested in helping me make a decision, so I was alone in this process. When I was about two or three months along, I decided that I would do the adoption. My aunt assured me that I would always see the baby at family gatherings and know that the child was okay. I went to Willis and told him what I was going to do, and he didn't care either way, so I said, "Good-bye, and thanks a lot." It would be almost nineteen years before he and I would speak again.

I told my aunt that I would let her adopt my child, and she made plans. She was very happy, and I was very sad. How did I get in this place again? Why did the men I care about not care back? I was deeply saddened. I went to the doctor regularly and found out the baby was a boy.

I told my aunt, and she made plans for a name. I just did what she wanted and tried to stay calm and sure, although I wasn't sure of anything. My aunts assured me I was doing the right thing.

I awoke one morning and knew that would be the day. I knew the baby boy would be born, and I was afraid. My friend took me to the hospital. The delivery was brief, and I don't remember the pain of birth—only the pain of knowing I wouldn't be taking this child home after all we had been through together. The child was taken from me at birth with the knowledge that there was an adoption coming.

Then it happened. The nurse brought the baby boy into my room to feed. I couldn't believe it! I picked him up, cried, told him I loved him, and talked to him as I fed him. I changed his diaper and rocked him to sleep. I gazed at my son and knew I would always have a place in my heart for him. I wondered if he would ever know me, find out about me, or want anything to do with me. I told him over and over that I loved him but that I didn't know how to take care of him. I asked him to forgive me. I cherished the time with him. I didn't tell the nurses, and they didn't ask. In my heart, I bonded with my son for the first two days of his life. I was allowed to care for him as a mother should even before his adopted mother could. I know today that was a gift from my Father in heaven. I felt the pain of saying good-bye to that baby.

I left the hospital two days later. I left with the baby and took him to his new parents. I was sad, and I cried. When we arrived at their home, I got out and took the baby in. His new mom was waiting in the back room, where the crib was. I handed her the baby. She was very happy and loved that baby from the moment he was in her arms. She told me, "Thank you," and promised me that she would take good care of him. She told me that God loved me and I needed to get my life right with Him. I told her I knew that to be true. I left without saying anything else. The ride home was painful. I cried all the way home. I had never experienced pain like that. The emptiness I felt in my heart and body was strong. I returned home to my oldest son and found comfort in his love for me. That is a day I will never forget.

Finally, I couldn't stand it anymore. I called my aunt and uncle to tell them I had changed my mind, and they would have to give the baby back to me. I couldn't do it. It hurt too much. But I got no answer. I tried for a couple of days. I called my other aunt and asked her why they weren't answering, and she told me that they took a month off to travel and show everybody their new son. I was crushed. I cried some more. My other aunt helped me through that time and saved us all from another choice. After a month, they were already attached to him. How could I tear him away from them? God touched my heart and allowed me to go on without my son. I didn't understand why I could let it go, but God had His mighty hand in the whole process. My only comfort was that I knew I would get to see him as he grew up because he was in my distant family. That hole was never filled, and it always ached in the quietness of my heart.

When Gabriel was about two years old, I was asked

to go to court to make the adoption legal. I went, and that was the first time I got to see him since he was born. He was everything a little two-year-old should be. He looked just like his father. He was curious, obedient, and cute. On the day of the adoption, Gabriel's last name was changed. I had named him what my aunt wanted, so the only name change he needed was his last name. Once again, I was given a special gift from God as I spent those days with Gabriel.

My aunt always let me have yearly pictures of Gabriel, so I got to watch him grow up in pictures. It seemed that he grew up really fast. He looked exactly like his father. I always received yearly milestones in his life. I remember when I found out that Gabriel was going to be a big brother. I thought they were going to adopt again, but I found out that his mom, my aunt, was pregnant. I was stunned. I thought she couldn't pregnant. My other aunt told me that his mom had RH negative blood and that with treatment, she was able to get pregnant. I was a little upset because the reason I gave Gabriel to them was because she couldn't get pregnant. I felt deceived and betrayed. I didn't know what to think. God touched my heart and let me know it was okay for Gabriel to have a sibling. He was alone and needed someone to grow up with. I felt gratitude again.

This adoptive family had suffered a lot of losses in a short time period. I went to funerals and saw Gabriel. At one family funeral, his mom came up to me with Gabriel and told him, "Gabriel, I want you to meet someone," and introduced me by name. Gabriel smiled and shook my hand; then his eyes got as big as saucers. He couldn't keep his eyes off me. I found out later that his mom had told him his real mother's name. By this time, he knew he was adopted and now for the first time, he met the mother, who gave birth to him. I couldn't keep my eyes off him either, but out of respect for Marsha, I didn't try to talk to him or spend time with him. I just watched him from afar.

My son's adoptive mom became very sick from diabetes, and went to another funeral with my aunt. She told me Gabriel's mom couldn't come because she was sick. We decided to go visit her. I had my oldest son with me. I hadn't told any of my children about Gabriel. The two boys hit it off really well that day. They took off to play basketball together and spent the whole visit together. I was overwhelmed that the two boys got along well at and after the visit. On the ride home, I told my oldest son the truth about Gabriel. I explained the whole situation to him. He seemed to understand and had few questions. He told me he liked Gabriel and that he liked that Gabriel was a good ball player.

One by one, I told all my children the truth about Gabriel, and they all were understanding and asked few questions. My daughter watched a lot of Oprah, and one day, she asked me if she was adopted. I assured her that she was not, but that was my opening to tell her about Gabriel. I told her that when I was younger, I adopted a child out. I told her about Gabriel. She crinkled her nose and asked, "You mean I have another brother?" She was the only girl with three brothers, and she was stunned to know that she had another brother. She then asked, "Are you sure you don't have a girl out there somewhere?" I assured her that I did not. She wanted to know if he knew about them, and I told her that he did. She wanted to know when they were all going to meet each other. I assured her that someday, they would. She seemed satisfied, and that was all that she said. I had no idea that day was just around the corner.

Gabriel's mom died in 2004. My kids and I went to the funeral. The kids wanted to buy a sympathy card for Gabriel, so we bought one, and everyone signed the card. I was the last to sign, and I read what each of the kids wrote. My heart jumped, and my eyes watered as I read the wonderful things those kids wrote to Gabriel. They all signed the card "your brother" and "your sister." How did I get to be the mom of such wonderful and accepting kids?

I knew of all that was going on in Gabriel's life. I knew when he graduated. I knew when he got married, and I knew when his wife had their first child. My aunt called and told me that Gabriel was a daddy and I was a grandma. I told my aunt to slow down. She laughed. I told her I was too young to be a grandma.

We went to the funeral. I was happy to see Gabriel, and I knew that the kids accepted him. I wouldn't disrespect his mom and try to get close to Gabriel while she was still alive, but I wondered what would happen now. I wanted Gabriel to know us and that we loved him. I told him that at the funeral. What I didn't expect was for his dad, Willis, to be there too. His dad went to Gabriel's graduation and wedding. I was upset because I wondered why he got to do that and I didn't get to. My aunt told me that Gabriel's dad's mom, Dena, was invited, and she always brought Gabriel's dad too. Still, I was a little resentful that he wouldn't help me make any decision about Gabriel but still reaped rewards. Something about that didn't seem right to me.

I didn't have time to dwell on that because I was going through my own stuff about Gabriel's dad and our unspoken past. We hadn't seen or spoken to each other in almost twenty years, and I didn't know what to do or say. I was afraid of everything about us.

My attention shifted to my kids wanting to talk with Gabriel. I introduced him to them, and they all gave him a big hug and offered their sympathies. He was grateful and happy that they talked to him. He read their card, and I could tell it meant a lot to him. He smiled in his grief.

At the service, the congregation waited for the immediate family to come in and be seated. Up to that point, I had not seen Gabriel's son. When we stood for the family, I saw Gabriel walk in with his son in his arms. As they walked in to sit down, his son looked at me, and I knew from that moment that we bonded in spirit. After the funeral, I went to see my grandson and hold him. He was curious about who I was. We had to work at our relationship because he didn't know who I was at that time. I didn't even have to touch my first grandson for us to bond. I only had to see him. This, too, is a special gift from my heavenly Father.

After the services at the cemetery, the guests and

family went back to the family home to eat. There we all got to visit, and family took a dozen pictures of all of us together. Gabriel's dad seemed quiet and reserved. I promised to keep in touch with the family. I told Gabriel that he was welcome if he wanted to get to know us and be a part of our family. He said that he would keep in touch. The day was long and ended with all of us saying good-bye and going our separate ways. I had no idea that part of my life had come full circle, and a whole new chapter had begun.

I felt many emotions. I was eight years sober. I was forty years old. I was somewhat disappointed that Gabriel's mom died when he was so young. His mom wasn't supposed to die. Gabriel needed her and experienced pain that he wasn't supposed to. What would Gabriel do? What about his dad? What about my grandson? Would Gabriel bring him to us? What about this? What about that? I couldn't put two thoughts together. I called my sponsor. She helped me get my bearings. It wasn't about me; it was about Gabriel and how I could help him.

Gabriel called me a few days later, and I invited him for a visit to our home. I agreed to come pick him up. It was almost a three-hour trip to get him, and I was worried about what he would say and ask me. But my worries quickly disappeared when we talked. He was calm, quiet, polite, and didn't ask many questions at all. He told me that his parents explained things to him when they told him about me, and they never spoke harshly of me. He knew his real dad and asked me about us. I told him that we really cared about each other, but I didn't know what happened between us either.

I got to know my grandson, who was about nine months old when Gabriel came home. I relished the title of Grandma to this little one, and he became the joy of my life. I took about a thousand pictures of him, and I wouldn't let anyone else hold or take care of him. All he needed was his grandma. He had free reign at my house. I never knew that I could love someone like I loved my children until my grandchildren came along. Those babies are right up there with their parents in my heart. What a wonderful joy grandchildren are. My grandson doesn't care what I look like, how much I weigh, or how I dress. He just cares that I love him. I was overwhelmed that Gabriel brought my first grandson into my life.

Some family members were a little upset that Gabriel came into my family so easily and felt that it was inappropriate for me to step in so quickly after his mom's death, but his mom stepped in for me when I needed her to, and I stepped in for her when she needed me to. Gabriel was only nineteen years old, and he still needed a mother. I talked with Gabriel's adopted dad, and he thought that Marsha wouldn't have it any other way. Gabriel is important in that matter. I make no apologies.

Gabriel was well-received into the family and got along well with his siblings, but it took him a while to find his place in the family. In his adoptive family, he was the only big brother, but when he came into my family, he was a big brother but not the oldest. His older brother and Gabriel bumped heads a time or two because big brother was and is the big brother to all of them, and he let Gabriel know that he was his big brother too.

Gabriel was delighted to have a sister. She received Gabriel well, and the two of them get along well. My two youngest children were always very close, and Jodie had to learn to share his sister with another brother. His sister has a good time teasing Gabriel and treats him the same as her other brothers. One year, one of my siblings came for Christmas and met Gabriel for the first time. I asked my brother what he thought about Gabriel and he said it seemed like he fit in well and seemed like he had always been there. God is good to me and my family. I know that God can fix what I have broken, and God can put it back together so well that you wouldn't even know it was broken in the first place.

Willis and I got a chance to talk on the phone about a favor for Gabriel's adoptive dad concerning Gabriel. We also had a chance to talk about the past. I found out what paralyzed Willis with fear about marrying me. My grandfather had caught us fooling around one day at home. He made me leave the home, and I had nowhere to go. Willis felt bad and said that I could stay with him at his parents' home. I agreed, and my son and I moved in there. I stayed a couple of months and found out that I was pregnant. We decided to get married. We made plans for the wedding. We were going to get married in the home at a small wedding with relatives and close friends. A family uncle was going to marry us. Then, my grandfather talked to his parents on the phone and told them that I was always fooling around with guys and that

I probably wasn't even pregnant by their son at all. They in turn told him.

I was stunned to hear that! I understood why everything fell apart so quickly, thoroughly, and completely. I went through a roller coaster of emotions. How could my grandfather say something like that? Why would he do that? I was angered and saddened that my grandfather destroyed a lot of lives with that lie. He couldn't stand to see anyone happy because he was a miserable soul. Willis and his parents believed the lie, and I was forced to make some hard decisions because of it.

Willis and I also talked about how our lives had turned out. He told me that he knew I had a drug and drinking problem. He blamed himself and wondered if he had caused it. I assured him that he didn't cause my drinking or drug problem and that I forgave him. We both reflected over what might have been. We knew we could never go back. We were saddened that we went our separate ways. Willis told me that when Gabriel was about two years old, his adoptive parents took Gabriel to the hospital when Willis's dad was dying. Matt, Willis's dad wanted to see Gabriel. It was here that Willis's parents knew without a doubt that Gabriel was their son's son. He looks exactly like their son but by now, everything was done.

So many people's happiness was destroyed because of a lie. How sad for the soul of the person who did that. But God is faithful. He allowed us all to come back together. It wasn't how we wanted or expected it, but we finally were able to talk, forgive, and experience some happiness in the way God puts back together what we break.

Today, my relationship with Gabriel is as strong as my relationships with the rest of my children. He calls me for advice, and I call him to see how he is doing. He is a vital part of this family and has found his place. He is still very close to his adoptive dad and keeps in contact with all his relatives. He had to learn the hard way the dos and don'ts of being one of my children. I had to correct and instruct him, and I have been so upset with him that I couldn't speak to him for fear of being unfair and spitting venom at him. But we have learned how to communicate with each other, and we both know we love each other. When I was upset with him, his brothers called him to warn him and let him know how to proceed with caution. I know he appreciated that. Gabriel has moved farther away, so I don't get to see him as much as the rest of the kids. When he gets a chance to come home, he does.

My life without Gabriel was hard. I cried many times and doubted and punished myself over and over. I lived in fear of being hated by a child I adopted out, but God has returned that child to me and my family, and he brought with him my oldest grandchild.

God restored my heart and restored our relationship. He gave Gabriel's love and forgiveness to me, and I love it when he calls me "Mom." I praise God for letting me know the son who came home.

6
The Child Who Loved So Much

Bug is my middle child and third son. He is the most loving son a mother could ever want. He is always happy to see me and always ends his conversations with "I love you." He is smart, handsome, and funny. He's caring and always had a compassionate spot in his heart. He cares for others naturally. He's determined and a hard worker. I call him the good son.

As parents of Bug, my husband and I never had any trouble from him. We didn't have driving troubles, girl troubles, drug or alcohol troubles, or school troubles with him. He was always obedient and wanted to please us. Looking at Bug, you would never know that he had some challenges in life that could have held him back. But these challenges did not hold back the child who loves so much.

When Bug was five or six months old, I laid him on

the floor on his stomach. He rose up on his tummy, and his arms and leg wiggled a lot. I thought he looked like a little bug. I started calling him that, and the name stuck with him ever since.

Bug was born on December 18, 1986. He was a low birth weight child, weighing only five pounds and fourteen ounces. The doctors induced my labor after the fluid test in my stomach showed he was ready to be born. He was born at 4:06 in the afternoon. It was a day that would change my life for the better.

The doctors induced my labor at noon. At 4:00, my water broke. Bug was born. I heard him cry and saw the doctors looking at him. But they kept looking at him. Then I remembered my dream. About two months earlier, I had a dream that scared me. I told my family there would be something different about Bug. In my dream, Bug was born, but the doctors wouldn't let me see him for about ten minutes. When they let me see him, I couldn't see his mouth. There was a gray space where his mouth was. I could see his eyes and nose but not his mouth. I woke up and was troubled by it. Now, in the hospital, my dream was playing out. Bug was born; the doctors wouldn't let me see him. When they did let me see him, something about his mouth was different. It was called a cleft palate.

The doctors said it was common. One in three children are born with one. I never saw one before, and my heart was stricken with fear. *How did that happen? Where did it come from? How did this happen to my child? Why did this happen?* I asked myself. The questions were endless.

My heart went to Bug, who I knew needed me more than anything. I was given a sedative. Bug was taken, and I went to sleep.

A nurse woke me to tell me there was someone who wanted to talk to me. I met a nice couple who had a son with them. They told me their son was born with a cleft palate and that he was fine. They told me about his surgeries that repaired his cleft palate. The son smiled and spoke to me. I thought, *As long as the doctors can repair the palate, I am okay, and Bug will be too.* I had no idea the hard work that lay ahead for Bug as well as our whole family.

Another nurse came in and told me I had to learn to feed Bug because he wasn't able to suck from a bottle. She showed me a bottle that had a one-inch tube on the end instead of a nipple. She said that I was to sit Bug up, lay the tube on his tongue, squeeze the milk onto his tongue, and he would swallow. Then they brought Bug to me. I held on to that little baby like life itself, and I squeezed him hard. The nurse smiled and said to try what she showed me. I sat Bug in my lap, put the tube on his tongue, squeezed the milk, and he swallowed. It went perfect. I thought, *This isn't so hard.* Bug was hungry. From birth, Bug had a great appetite. He drank the milk well. I was already very proud of him. He was beautiful, and I could see that he was strong and determined.

Most of my hospital stay was spent learning all that Bug needed. Bug was low in weight, and the doctors worried that he needed extra nourishment, so he was given special milk to help him gain the weight he needed for his first surgery, which would be in three months. He needed to weigh at least ten pounds. He needed to double his weight.

We left the hospital after a few days with an appointment at the children's hospital in two weeks. I had a lot of hard work to get Bug where he needed to be to start his journey through surgeries.

Bug's older brother, B, was very happy to see Bug. He never asked about Bug's mouth. He loved Bug from the first time he saw him. I laid Bug in his crib and took a bath, and Bug's big brother was so happy to spend time with him. He used to call Bug "Boogersnot." He talked to Bug and always wanted to play with him. It has always been this way with Bug. Once Bug's love gets a hold of you, you can only love him.

I decided to give Bug my breast milk as well as the other milk to help Bug make his weight. Bug had breast milk and low birth weight milk and regular formula milk after a month. Bug was well above the weight he needed when he had his first surgery.

In two weeks, I went to the Oral/Maxillofacial Surgery Clinic, and there I saw the one in three kids born with a cleft palate. My heart was stunned by all these beautiful children with different degrees of cleft palates. Some were severe and some not. One small girl had no nose, and I was saddened to think of her future. All I knew was they were there to have surgeries. I met a woman, and we chatted for a while. She was there with her kids. She had six of them. All of them had cleft palates. She said they were all adopted because they were given up by their parents. I couldn't even think of that. My Bug needed me more than anything, and he depended on me. We were on this journey together.

Our family went to visit one of our family friends. This friend had a sister who was visiting. She saw Bug and was moved to hold him. She took him into the bedroom and started praying for him, and then she started speaking in tongues over Bug. This went on for quite some time. She was crying and filled with the Holy Ghost. Afterward, she told us that the Holy Spirit told her that Bug would have a tough beginning in life but that he was strong. He would grow up to be a great advisor to many, and everything he touched would turn to gold. She said that he would grow up to be loved by everyone, had special abilities, and carried a special gift. She said that he would become great in our family. That came true in the life of Bug and in our family. He became that and much more.

Bug's first surgery was scheduled. The surgery was to close his upper lip from the double split to the part of his lip that was there and to put in the palate that the doctors made for him to serve as a palate until they made one for him. Dr. L told us that the surgery would take about an hour and a half, and the only reason that it would take longer was if there was a problem. The doctors were pleased with Bug's weight.

The nurse came and got Bug, and we waited. I was sick with worry. I wanted to cry. Two and a half hours after the surgery started, I was frantic. *Something must be wrong.* My mind flashed to my baby. I wanted to see Bug. I knew he needed me. What was going on? Finally,

Dr. L came out and told us that everything went well and that he took extra time on Bug to be more detailed in his surgery. He said that Bug had good skin that was workable, and the extra detail would hopefully prevent more surgery in the future. I didn't know how important that would be in the future. I let the doctor know that I was upset because the surgery had taken so long. He smiled and apologized. Then he took me see Bug.

Dr. L tried to prepare me for what I was going to see, but I nearly fainted when I saw Bug. My poor baby had stitches and yellow stuff all over his face, and I could tell that he had been crying. His eyes were swollen and puffy. His mouth was different. His lip was closed, but it looked painful. I fell to my knees and started crying. The nurses had to help me out of the room because they were afraid that I might scare Bug. I pulled myself together quickly. I knew he needed me. The nurse wanted me to hold Bug so that he would feel familiar touch and his stress would be lessened. I couldn't upset Bug. I knew he needed me, and I had to put my own fear aside and be strong for him. There were other surgeries, and I couldn't behave this way.

I collected myself and went to Bug. I loved Bug very much. I just sat there and held him. I rocked him and prayed for him. I talked to him and let him know I was there and that everything was going to be all right. Bug did well. Soon after surgery, he had a bottle—the same kind he always used—but the nurse said that in a week, he would be able to use a regular bottle. She showed me the plastic palate in his mouth. I was amazed at the process of repairing the palate. Bug also had nose packs that would open his nostrils while the lip healed. Bug also had a bow across his lip called a Logan's' Bow to protect his lip from being touched by anything.

Bug was sent home in a few days with arm pads to keep from touching his face. It was good to see Bug use a regular nipple on his bottle. As instructed, I pulled out the palate and turned this little screw in the middle of it every day. This was to widen his bone in his mouth for when the doctors did bone grafts for the palate from his own bone when he got older. He didn't like us taking the palate out, but we did it. Bug was always happy and smiled all the time. He always wanted to do something. He learned to walk at nine months so he could follow his big brother around the house. Bug healed well.

Bug was about a year and a half old when he needed another surgery. Bug grew slower than other children his age, and sometimes, that prevented him from having surgery because the doctors didn't want to do something and have to go back and do it again because Bug had outgrown it. This stalled Bug's surgeries for a while. Bug needed to have a piece of skin put in that separated his nose from his lip. As he grew, his lip pulled his nose flat. Another surgery was scheduled, and skin was taken from Bug's hip and used to make the repair. This time, I handled the surgery much better, and Bug coasted along with the same beautiful smile on his face.

Bug was sent home with instructions to not let anything touch his lip. We put antibiotic creams on his lip to help heal the stitches. We were told to make sure he didn't bump his mouth on anything. That was easy for them to say and sounded fine in theory, but Bug was an on-the-go kid with places to go and things to get into. I was a nervous wreck, trying to keep track of him and his brother. Then it happened. Bug was running and fell and hit his lip in the edge of the coffee table, and blood went everywhere. I was frantic. I was also pregnant again. I yelled for my son to get in the car, and we rushed to the emergency room. I was frantic and told the doctors about Bug surgery's, which they didn't know about. The staff didn't know what to do, so they paged Dr. L, and we waited while we heard from the doctor.

When Dr. L arrived, it looked like he had been playing basketball. He immediately came when he heard that Bug was in the emergency room. The surgery was a week old. He looked at Bug, cleaned up his mouth, and said that everything was all right. Bug had not split open the stitches, but he would have more bruising, and there would be more swelling. But he was okay. I thanked the doctor for coming, and he reassured me that Bug was special to him, and he would always show up if Bug needed him. Bug has always had that effect on people. Dr. L had hundreds of patients, but there was something special about Bug, and the doctor knew it.

Bug started school. I put him into Head Start because I wanted him to have advantages in school. He did well, and then he started kindergarten. My kids went to the same elementary school that I went to. Their school principle was one of my sixth-grade teachers, Mr. E. I took Bug to school and showed him around. I showed him where his class would be. I showed him the cafeteria and told him that was where he would eat lunch. I showed him the gym and told him he would play games in there. I showed him where his brother's class would be. I wanted him to feel comfortable and not be scared of school. I didn't have to worry; the school did!

I got a call from school about two weeks into the school year. To my horror, the teacher had lost Bug. She didn't know where he was, and she was frantic. By the time I got to school, there was an all-out search for him. I asked questions, and then I remembered the cafeteria. I looked in there and saw Bug eating. I went to him and asked him why he wasn't in class. He said, "Mama, you told me this is where to go to eat, and I was hungry." The teacher was happy to find him. I explained to him that he didn't get to eat lunch in kindergarten. Soon after that, I got another call. Bug was gone again. He wasn't in the cafeteria this time. The search was on. Bug was found in the gym this time. He wanted to play. I explained to him that he didn't get to play in the gym in kindergarten. I would like to say that this was the last time Bug left his class, but it wasn't. I got another call. Bug walked out to find his brother. He made it all the way to the sixth-grade hall and went into his brother's class. It was incredible that he remembered the class from when I showed him around several weeks before. To the teacher's surprise, big brother brought Bug back to class. The teacher hadn't missed him yet.

The popcorn lady was a friend of our family, and the popcorn machine was just outside Bug's class. He got up when he smelled the popcorn, got a bag from the popcorn lady, and came back to class with a bag of popcorn. Again, I explained that you could only have popcorn when everyone else in class did. The next time, he tried to bring bags of popcorn into the class for everyone. Bug wore out Mrs. R, his kindergarten teacher, and Mr. E. Bug finished kindergarten, but I put him into pre-first grade. I felt like he spent the whole kindergarten year trying to adjust to the don'ts. He let me know that he didn't like kindergarten because he didn't get to do anything fun. He was glad to get out of kindergarten.

This is where things get a little fuzzy for me. Somewhere in these years, Bug had a bone graft to put bone in the top of his mouth to replace the plastic palate that was there. Bone was taken from his hip and put into his mouth to make a roof for his mouth. The bone would then fuse together to make a palate. I do not remember where or when this was done. I was heavy into my drinking, but I know it was done while he was little.

When Bug was six, he was diagnosed with ADD. The doctor wanted to give him some medication for it. His father and I said no to medicine, that somehow Bug needed to release all that energy somewhere positive. We put him in soccer. Bug played soccer for a couple of seasons. He really liked it, although he didn't understand the game at first. He loved to kick the ball and run. He didn't like to play goalie because he had to stay in one place. But when the other team made a point because Bug wasn't guarding the goal, I told him how he let his team down. He didn't like that. I told him that everyone had to play goalie on the team, and when it was his turn, he was to try his best to not let his team down. He didn't ever let a ball get by him again. He still didn't like to play goalie, but he did for the team. He's always been like that, he'll work harder for a team than for himself.

Bug was the kind of kid who would talk to anyone at any time. I talked to my kids about talking to strangers and told them that if they ever got lost to go to a policeman and tell him their names and that they were lost. I talked to Bug a lot about that. He was always hard to keep track of. One time, after a soccer game, my family went to the flea market. It was Saturday and busy, and we shopped and walked around. Just as I noticed that Bug was missing, I heard over the intercom, "Mr. and Mrs. Stoner, please come to the front door. We have Bug, and you are lost."

We hurried to the front door, and there was Bug, sitting on a stool, crying. When he saw me, he jumped down, ran over to me, and said, "I did what you told me to, Mommy. I did what you told me to." I said, "That's good, Bug, and you got found, didn't you?" He nodded his head and gave me a big hug. Bug stayed close to me after that when we went places. He was six years old.

Bug was always curious and mischievous. Once, we went shopping at the grocery store. Bug started crying and rubbing his mouth. I thought he had fallen and hurt his mouth, but he said that he didn't. He wanted something to drink. When I got him something, he didn't drink it; he poured it on his hand and rubbed it on his face. I didn't know what was wrong. But he cried and rubbed his face with the ice. I thought, *What did he get into?* I asked him,

"Bug, did you eat something in the store?" He nodded his head. I had to think. Then it hit me—Bug bit into a jalapeno pepper, and it burned his mouth.

A lady on our street had house plants in her front window. I ran to her house when we got home and asked her if she had an aloe vera plant. She said no and asked me why. I told her about Bug, and she gave me something else called melaleuca. It was oil for burns. I thanked her and ran home to put it on Bug's mouth and chin. I was afraid that he would have blisters. I rubbed the oil on, and it stopped the burn. I was happy, and so was Bug. I told Bug to not eat things if he didn't know what they were. To this day, Bug hates hot or spicy food. So it was for the child who loved so much. There was never a dull moment!

I left my marriage in 1996. I moved to another city. During this time, Bug got into a children's hospital program in Texas and had his first surgery in this hospital. Skin was removed from Bug's hip, and a soft palate was put into his throat. This surgery was difficult for him. It took longer to heal, but as usual, Bug came out of this surgery with flying colors. He is a miracle. He has always had a high tolerance for pain. It took him a while to learn to use the flap in the back of his throat.

Since Bug started speaking, he was in speech therapy. This continued until Bug was in high school. He was always determined and committed. Today, he speaks very well and loves to talk. He has no problem being understood and has no trouble saying any words or phrases. I commend all the teachers who were committed to help Bug.

Bug continued his surgeries in Texas. In the next surgery, two teeth that were imbedded in the roof of his mouth were pulled out. We traveled to Texas for surgery. This was the first time I went to the Children's Hospital, and I was struck by the magnitude of their services for the children and families of those they help. This is a nonprofit organization, and their facilities were fabulous. This hospital helped kids with cleft palates and burn victims. This children's hospital gave you money if you drove yourself or transported you and your child via van to any of its hospitals. The hospital put parents and their children up in a motel and got them to and from the hospital. They were great. The hospital always had two drivers to a van and rotated drivers during the trip.

Bug went through his surgery with the ease that he always did, but one time, he was in a room next to a boy who was about two years old, and the boy cried all the time. Bug was struck with that crying and asked me what was wrong with the little boy. I asked the nurse, she told me, and I told Bug. Bug got up, went to the boy's bed, and said, "Hi. My name is Bug. What's your name?" Bug laid his hand on the boy's head and spoke gently to him. For the first time in two days, the boy stopped crying. Bug did this from time to time until we left, and the boy always stopped crying. When it was time for Bug to leave, he went to the boy and told him that he was leaving. He gave the boy a pat on the head and spoke kindly to him. We turned to leave the room.

I had made Bug a fleece blanket that he took to the hospital when he had surgeries. As we were leaving, he stopped and went back to the boy. He spoke to the boy, put his blanket on the boy, and smiled. He pulled the blanket up to the boy's neck, for the boy could not do that for himself; his arms and legs had been burned off. I cried because I had a child who loved so much that he would forget his own pain and leave something that brought him comfort for someone who needed it more that he did. I hugged him and told him how nice that was. He said, "Mom, if that blanket made me feel better, maybe it will make him feel better." He hoped the little boy would be okay. The child who loved so much touched someone's life in a great way. I was very proud of him.

By now, Bug was in junior high school. He played football and wrestled. He was behind in school, but my husband and I put him in summer school and a summer tutoring program with for a couple of years. Bug did well there and got caught up in school. He liked the tutoring and told me that they made learning English and Math easy for him to understand. He did well from then on in school. He was often chosen as an outstanding student in that summer program. He was eager to help others. He always cheered for the underdog and the kids who nobody liked and were picked on. He always took up for them and became friends with them. He told me, "I know what it's like to get picked on and teased, and I don't like it, and I know that they don't either." One time, Bug told me that a guy teased him at school for having a cleft lip, and I burned with anger. But not Bug. He said he didn't care, but I knew that it hurt him. I wanted to beat the boy up myself for teasing my son, but Bug talked me out of it. Bug always kept those things to himself because he knew they would hurt my feelings. The child who loved so much wouldn't let that kind of stuff hurt his mama.

The next surgery was to close the small hole left from the bone graft. It was in the roof of Bug's mouth. Once again, we traveled to the Children's Hospital. Bug's sister wanted to go with me to stay in the hospital to help me care for Bug. This surgery was easy. Bug always had great healing ability, and this surgery was no different. We stayed in the hospital for a week, and his sister and I took turns sleeping and caring for Bug when he needed something like an extra blanket, a drink of water, or to go to the bathroom.

At this time, Bug needed braces, and the waiting list for braces was about two years. My husband and I decided to have the braces put on in our hometown. The doctors said that would be okay, and they would work in a team with the orthodontist of our choice. We found a dentist, and the work began. Bug told me that he hated tightening those braces. He said it was painful, but he did it. He had to keep wax with him to keep the braces from rubbing sores on the inside of his mouth. He wore them for two years and had a retainer that we replaced a couple of times. Once, while he was eating at a restaurant, he laid the retainer on a napkin. While he was eating, the waitress took the napkin, thinking it was trash, and threw it away.

Bug had one more surgery that was purely cosmetic. I wanted him to have it, but Bug was done and didn't want to have it. At the time the surgery was scheduled, he was eighteen years old and could make his own choice, and he chose not to have the last one. I knew he wouldn't change his mind, and I thought, *If Bug is done, then we're done.* Bug had a total of six surgeries. The doctors at the Children's Hospital were impressed that Bug only needed six surgeries. Bug had a severe cleft palate, and usually double-digit surgeries were needed to repair it, but God looked upon Bug, and he didn't need that many. Bug never needed surgeries to repair the scar tissue on his mouth. I had heard about cocoa butter healing scars, so I bought a tube of pure cocoa butter and told Bug to rub that on his lip as many times as he wanted so he wouldn't have a red, thick scar. Bug began shaving at an early age so hair would grow on his upper lip. Bug never needed any tubes in his ears either.

At the Children's Hospital, I learned what a good job Dr. L did for Bug. The doctors there were impressed that Bug's lip and nose were so aligned so well. They told me that Bug's first surgeon took great care to put those together so well. I realized why that first surgery took so long. It all started with that first repair, and Dr. L did a hero's job. I decided that we needed to find Dr. L. I made some calls and located him. I called and made an appointment, and Bug and I went to see him. Bug was sixteen years old, and Dr. L hadn't seen him in almost twelve years. Dr. L was happy to see Bug. He told his nurses about Bug and took pictures. Bug was somewhat quiet and didn't really remember Dr. L, but that didn't matter. We talked of what had happened to Bug and where he had completed his surgeries.

Dr. L was happy that Bug did so well. He was surprised that only a few surgeries were needed. I got a chance to thank the doctor who took such great care with the child who loved so much. Dr. L said Bug's speech was great and was totally in awe of Bug. Dr. L had tears in his eyes as we talked of all the old times together. As we left the office, we noticed that Dr. L had a picture of Bug smiling as his screen saver. Dr. L thanked us for coming and told us that Bug was always special to him. He was glad to know that his hard work had helped Bug immensely in the long run. We went away from that meeting with a strong feeling thankfulness to that doctor.

Bug is done with his surgeries and has had seven surgeries to date. He is happy. He finished high school and works for United Airlines. He moved out of the home six years ago. I was lost without the child who loves so much. He was always there to greet me at the door when I got home and say good-bye to me when I left home. He always wanted to talk to me and asked me if I wanted anything. He was always happy to see me and said, "Hi, Mommy!" I love that about him.

I miss Bug very much, but I get to see him at work because I work at the airport too. My friend, at work, told me that whenever I see Bug, my eyes light up and I get a big smile on my face. She also told me that I can spot Bug a mile away. I told her it's because his heart is so big, I can't miss it.

Bug became what the lady who spoke in tongues said he would become, and he is only twenty-eight years old. He has much to give, and I look forward to seeing what else the child who loves so much will do with his life. He is close to his brothers and sisters and to me. He keeps in touch with all of his family, as he should. Bug graduated in 2006. I was happy to see him in his cap and gown. He did it! I knew he could.

Bug told me that the guy who used to tease him apologized to him. Bug saw the guy somewhere, and he said, "Hey, Bug," like they were old friends. Bug said hi back. Bug was taken aback because this boy gave Bug a hard time in school and teased him about his mouth. Now he acted like they were old friends. Bug reminded him of how he used to tease him, and the boy—now a young man too—didn't remember but told Bug he was sorry. They left each other as friends. When Bug told me this, I thought, *Good, now I can take him off the hit list.*

So it is with the child who loves so much. He just forgave the guy and went on. I wish I had half the courage and fortitude that Bug has. He went through a lot, and still, his greatest gift is to love others.

I am honored to be chosen to be the mother of the child who loves so much. Bug has given me wonderful gifts as we journeyed this road together. I have learned a lot about life, Bug, and myself.

God truly blessed me, and I will always love the child who loves so much. He showed me how to love and forgive and accept others. I am thankful to God for His faithfulness in our lives!

7
Mr. W

Jodie was born on New Year's Day at 11:57 a.m. He is the youngest of my five children.

Jodie has always been a happy child. He has the best smile. He has dimples that he got from me. He was always *very* smart and *very* good at math. He and his sister are eleven months and three weeks apart. Everyone thought they were twins as they grew up. Jodie has always been the baby of our family and always will be.

I always enjoyed Jodie as a child, although he always seemed to live within himself. He was always fine being by himself. As the kids grew up and started going to school and Jodie was left alone, he was okay with that. He liked his mama time.

As a young mother with five children, I was always out of sorts. When I spoke to the kids or a particular child, I called them the wrong names. After we *moved* to a new house, the kids were outside talking to the kids in the neighborhood, I saw Bug, Jodie's older brother by two years, grab Jodie by the collar and bring him into the house. He said, "Mama, those kids asked Jodie what his name was, and he told them his oldest brother's name—his other brother's name—then Jodie."

I told Jodie, "That's not your name."

He asked, "It isn't? What's my name?"

I told him, "Jodie W." From then on, he would say, "My name is Jodie W." He always said both names. We still laugh at that.

Jodie and his sister were always close. They did everything together. I used to call them partners in crime. No matter where one was, the other was there. They used to play the game Memory together. Jodie was *very* good at the game. He tried to tell his sister where the match was, but she *never* listened, and he always won. When he was about four or five years old, I told him a quarter was twenty-five cents. Then I asked him how many quarters would make one dollar, or one hundred cents. He thought about it and said it would take four quarters to make one hundred cents. I didn't realize he knew the concept of math or adding. He told me later that math was his favorite subject in school.

I made the kids go to bed at the same time, except my oldest, who was seven years older. One time, Jodie just wouldn't go to sleep. He wanted to watch TV with me. I was watching a scary movie called *Arachnophobia*. I told him he had to watch that movie with me if he wanted to stay up. I told him it was scary. He agreed. Jodie used to (and still does) *love* lizards, worms, and bugs. He always had dead things or Hot Wheels in his pants pockets when I did laundry. He wasn't afraid of any kind of bug or spider. When he was about five years old, he caught a grass snake and wanted to keep it, and we did. We kept it in an aquarium until I got up one night and saw the snake trying to get out. He caught a horny toad, and we kept that until it was gone from the box. A friend caught a salamander once by accidentally stepping on its foot and injuring it, and Jodie kept that too. He loved reptiles and bugs. As we started watching the spider movie together, we had a pit group, and Jodie sat on the other end. As the movie progressed, he got closer to me, and by the end of the movie, he was on my lap. He watched the whole movie, and he is scared of spiders to this day! A few days later, Jodie started yelling, screaming, and jumping all over the place. We asked him, "What the heck is wrong with you?"

Jodie stopped and said, "I thought a spider was on me!"

I said, "Dang, boy!" We still laugh at that.

Jodie always wanted me to buy him an iguana from the time he was about five years old. He wanted to name the iguana Doug. When Joseph was nineteen years old, I bought him a stuffed iguana and made a name tag with Doug on it and gave it to Joseph for Christmas. When he opened the gift, he told me he almost started crying. He couldn't believe I remembered he wanted an iguana named Doug. Doug rides in Jodie's car.

Once, I came home from work and used the bathroom. I got mad because the toilet wouldn't flush. I came out and asked for all the kids to come to me. All the kids came to the bathroom. I said I was mad because the toilet wasn't flushing, and I told the kids that someone was using too much toilet paper. Jodie said, "It ain't me, Mom; I don't use toilet paper!"

I asked, "What?" Jodie was five at the time. We laugh at that too. Jodie was always like that. He said and did funny things without trying.

We lived in a house by a creek. Jodie was home alone with me because he wasn't old enough to go to school yet. He talked to someone. I heard him talking and laughing. I asked him who he was talking to, and he said, "This girl." He said her name was Friendly. No one could see her but him, and she was with him often. My oldest son told me things he heard and saw at that house. One night, I heard something strange. I talked to the landlord and asked her if anything bad happened in the house before we moved in. She asked me why, and I told her the things we heard. She told me that a lady was beaten to death in that house by her ex-husband. Her name was Francis! Jodie's friend was a girl named Friendly. I think he didn't know how to say her name, so he called her that. I recently asked him if he remembered Friendly, and he said he didn't. I'm just glad she was nice to him.

Jodie did well in his younger years, but when his father and I separated and I went to detox, he returned to me very different. He was rebellious and angry. He didn't do well in school anymore. The divorce and me leaving to get sober hurt him the most. He was the youngest, and he felt alone. He was always closer to me than his dad, and he had just started school. During the four years, he didn't progress much emotionally. No one took the time to help him with his difficulties, and he just didn't know what was bothering him and how to talk to anyone.

Jodie came to live with me after I remarried. Jodie was angry, and he and I went around and around. He had just turned ten. He got caught stealing at the mall and had to go to a court of his peers. He didn't like it and had to pay restitution for his theft. He chose to hang out with some pretty rebellious guys and thought he could do whatever he wanted. He was wrong, and he and I went around and around for several years. But he learned not to steal. Praise the Lord.

I always knew the divorce hurt Jodie, but I didn't allow that to be an excuse for getting in trouble—and that went for all my children. He was gifted and smart and could succeed in every way, but he chose to succeed in the lower things. I was often called to the school because of problems there. Once, Jodie was in trouble for talking back to a security guard, and I had to pick him up. The principal told me that Jodie was doing something, and the guard told him to stop. Jodie didn't. The guard asked him his name, and Jodie told him. The guard kept talking to him, and then Jodie asked the guard his name. The guard said his name, and Jodie told the guard if he, Jodie, had to call him, the guard, by his last name, then the guard needed to address him as "Mr. W" as well! He was in more trouble for wanting to be addressed as Mr. W. My family gets a kick out of that, and that has been his name ever since. When someone asks about Mr. W, they are referring to Jodie.

Jodie was always a good athlete. He played basketball, soccer, and ran track. The 800 meters was his favorite event. He also did the long jump. Jodie played on a soccer team called the Titans, a local team of twelve- and thirteen-year-olds. Jodie was good and sometimes got after his teammates for their mistakes. Sometimes, he wasn't nice about it. I told him that not everyone was a natural athlete like he was. One time at practice, I heard Jodie having words with his coach. Jodie didn't want to do what the coach asked him. I was not happy with Jodie. I called to him, and we left. He told me he couldn't leave because practice wasn't over yet. I told him it didn't matter because he wasn't practicing anyway. I didn't allow him to play in the next game. He wondered why, and I told him, "When you don't practice, you don't play." He didn't like it, and I didn't care.

I told my kids that sports were an extra enjoyment, and if they thought I was supposed to let them play, they were wrong. A couple of weeks later, I heard Jodie tell the coach no. This time, we left practice, went home, and got his uniform. He asked me why, and I didn't say. We took his uniform to his coach and turned it in. The coach and Jodie begged me to let him play. They had an important game coming up, but I said no. I waited for him to miss the game before we talked about why he wasn't allowed to play on the team anymore. I needed him to understand that he was to listen to the coach. He was to practice when it was practice time. If he chose to continue to be a bad sportsman, he would not play—ever! I told him it hurt me that he didn't play but that it hurt me more to see that he didn't know how to be a good sportsman and teammate. He finally got the message. The coach and the team had no more trouble from him. His team won the state championship in its age group that year. He played in the game, got a trophy, and was in the championship picture.

Jodie was a good runner and could run far. He got that ability from me. I used to run cross-country in high school. I couldn't run fast, but I could run far. Jodie was the same way. He used to compete at school and was invited to run at a meet where the winners were invited to the Hershey Invitational in Pennsylvania to compete nationally. We traveled to Norman for the qualifying track meet. We waited for his event, the 800 meters. The 800-meter event is two laps around the track. He seemed calm and confident. When the race started, Jodie was in lane four. They were off. By the end of the first lap, he was in third place. He took off and passed the second guy, who was giving out. At the 220-yard marker, he tried to pass the first guy. Jodie always saved some for the last stretch, and he kicked in and passed to take the lead with 50 yards left. He hit the tape, and we went wild. He placed first, and we knew he was on his way to Hershey. He was very happy. He got a medal, and his oldest brother carried him on his shoulders. It was a good day.

We waited all week for a call to come to Hershey. Finally, I called the meet committee and found out that a guy from the Texas Invitational had beat Jodie's time by one-tenth of a second. Jodie wasn't going to Hershey. I had to tell him. He was disappointed, and so was the rest of the family. But he was still our champion and the state champion in the 800 meters that year. We were still proud of him. He ran hard and did a good job. He was disappointed but didn't let the loss keep him down for long.

Jodie continued to run and play soccer until one day he hurt his ankle in a game. We took him to the doctor, and the doctor couldn't tell what was wrong. It wasn't broken. We went to several doctors, and none could tell us what was wrong. He wore a boot for many weeks, and finally, he just stopped wearing it. This went on for a year. His ankle hurt, and he couldn't play ball or run like he used to. When he did run, it was painful. One day, he was at our family chiropractor. The doctor saw Jodie's ankle wrapped and asked what was wrong. Jodie told him he didn't know. The doctor un-wrapped it, looked at it, said it was dislocated, and popped it in three different places. The pain was gone, but since he had gone so long with it out of place, his ankle became stiff and was never the same.

Jodie worked a couple of summers as a lifeguard. He took the CPR class and then the lifeguard class. When I picked him up on test day, I asked him if he passed, and he said he didn't want to talk about it. I thought he didn't pass, and I started to feel bad. He smiled, laughed, and said that he passed. He always joked like that. He worked several summers at the neighborhood pool. I went to the pool, and my grandson would see Jodie and yell at him,

"Uncle Jo Jo." That is his name to his nephews. Jodie saw him and came over to play with him in the water. Uncle Jo Jo is this grandson's favorite uncle. It was a joy to see him work and earn honest money, and he was good at it. I laughed because the little girls at the pool said, "Hi, lifeguard," to him. Then they got woozy and silly and screamed when he said hi back to them.

During his high school years, Jodie had to learn everything the hard way. He just wouldn't listen—at least, not to anyone who cared for him. Jodie met a girl in high school, and she was by his side through the good and bad times of his teenage years. Jodie wouldn't keep a job and didn't feel like he needed to go to school. He had his friends, and that was all he needed. I could feel my son slipping into the abyss of rebellion. He missed so many classes when he was sent to detention or skipped school that he was years behind in school. The school contacted me. Jodie had to leave school because he was so far behind. I knew he was disappointed.

I went to pick Jodie up from school. I prayed and asked God to give me the right encouraging words to say to him. I told him that he was going to get a GED. I paid for the test and sent him to the classes with encouragement. I knew he could pass the test. Jodie was smart. He just seemed to use his smarts in a wrong and destructive way. Jodie passed the test with high scores. I was proud of him and prayed for his life. He realized later that he could have done much better in those days. I told my children as they grew up that they only got one chance to do it right, and all they had to do was go to school.

Jodie let me know that because he was the youngest, I forgot to include him in any kind of information. I forgot to tell him what I told the others about chores and how-to's and why's. Sometimes he wouldn't do his chores. Finally, I asked him why he didn't start the dishwasher like I asked him to. He told me he didn't know how to. I asked, "What do you mean you don't know how to start the dishwasher?" He told me that I told everybody else and showed them how to use the washer, dryer, and dishwasher, but I forgot to tell him. I showed him how to use all the appliances, and things were better. I didn't realize that I left him out, and he didn't say. Now I make sure he knows what everybody else knows. Because he was the baby of the family. I had to tell his brothers and sister to stop doing everything for him when he was little. They tied his shoes for him all the time. I made them stop doing things for him so he could learn on his own. I had to tell his sister to stop cutting his fingernails. Jodie was sixteen years old at the time.

I have learned a lot from and about Jodie. He is still funny and bright. He is still with his high school sweetheart. He lived with his brother, Bug, for several years. Bug helped him learn to go to work every day. Jodie is coming into adulthood. He is finding his worth and finding out family will always be there. His friends and some of the people in life will come and go but not family. Family will always be there for him. I still tell him to pray and thank God for all his blessings. He does.

In the summer of 2010, I was worried about Jodie finding his way in life. God spoke to me and let me know that Jodie would be a preacher someday. I thanked God for this revelation and for allowing my son to become a preacher. There has never been a preacher in the W. family, and I asked the Lord if I could live long enough to see this happen in the life of my youngest son.

It was my birthday, and all the kids were at my house. They were waiting for me to get home from work so we could go to dinner as a family. I talked with Jodie about getting a job. He couldn't get a job because he smoked pot. I asked Jodie why he smoked pot if it kept him from getting a job, and he said that he smoked pot to deal with his pain. I asked, "What pain?" He told me his ankle, knee, and hip hurt from his ankle injury years before.

I could tell he was depressed. He said, "Yes, Mom. I'm giving up." I became angry and knew that he was being attacked by Satan. Satan knew that Jodie was going to be a preacher, so he attacked Jodie's mind, body, and spirit. I claimed victory in Jodie's life through prayer until he could claim it for himself. I let Satan know that he couldn't have Jodie. Jodie was saved in 2005. God has a plan for Jodie's life. I knew Jodie needed help. I talked with a friend from work and asked him to come and pray over Jodie and anoint him with oil. We set a date, and I asked all the kids to be there. I told them we would have a family dinner. I also asked everyone to think of things they admire about Jodie and things they could thank him for in their lives—things he gave them. They agreed, and we planned to uplift him as a family.

Sunday came, and everyone was there. My friend

talked and shared Scripture with Jodie. He told him the story about Joseph in the Bible. That is Jodie's favorite Bible story. Before my friend anointed Jodie with oil, the family formed a circle around Jodie and then told him how we admired him and what we were thankful for about him. We cried and laughed as a family. Then my friend prayed for Jodie and anointed him. It was moving, and from that day on, Jodie stood a foot taller in stature. We wanted him to know that we as a family didn't hold him to his mistakes. We wanted him to see how we really saw him as a son, brother, family member, and person. We wanted him to know how much we admired and loved him and that he was an important, necessary member of the family. I was amazed at how his brothers and sisters saw him too. The talk was just what he needed.

Jodie married his high school sweetheart in September 2011. He is working a good job and is happy. I am happy the Lord spared Jodie's life through his difficult youth and destructive choices. I know God's will is going to be done in his life.

Mr. W and his wife let us know they are expecting a child in August 2013. Jodie called me and was very happy! My eyes teared up, and I listened on the phone to my youngest son talk about how happy he was to become a father. He has plans to work more and give his child what he or she needs in life. I reminded him to tell his wife how beautiful she is and that her body will change when she gives birth to their child. He said, "Okay, Mom," and thanked me for my help in his life. I told him to always remember to thank God for answered prayer in his life and to always be thankful for his blessings. I am thankful to God for His faithfulness in the life of Jodie and lives of those I love.

8

The Alfa

In November 1996, I moved to a new city. I moved here to live in a halfway house called 12 and 12 for people in recovery. This facility had detox, treatment, and halfway living for men and women. I was thirty-two years old, and I had just completed twenty-eight days of treatment in a small town. I felt hopeful but uncertain of my future. I wanted to stay sober, and I couldn't go back to the way I had been living for the past twelve years. I had left my children with family and gone to detox and then treatment, and I was going to live in a halfway house for women. I had never lived outside of my hometown.

I was afraid I had made the wrong choice when I checked in to 12 and 12. Everything was matter-of-fact, and there wasn't much time to talk about me. I had never lived with women and didn't like the prospect very much. I met the tech who checked me in and went through my property. I was assigned a room. I was given a sheet with the rules on it. I would meet my counselor the following week. I would have to get a job to pay for my living at 12 and 12. I started to not feel good about my choice to come there. I had never previously had to work to live somewhere.

My roommate helped me get a job making pizza at a pizza place. I started going to twelve-step meetings at this center. I started meeting some of the women. I met my counselor the next week. I thought she was pretty and too young to have a drinking or drug problem. I started falling into a routine of work and meetings, signing in and signing out.

I was married at this time, and my husband was upset that I didn't return home. He knew where I was and kept calling me and telling me to come home. I just couldn't at the time. I had just gotten a taste of something I never had before, and I wanted to stay sober.

I didn't come to this place to meet someone new. I didn't come for any reason except to learn a new way of life. I wanted to live a life without drugs, drinking, and abuse.

I met lots of people, and everyone seemed to want the same things. Everyone seemed to be headed in the same direction. Everyone went to meetings and talked recovery. I loved this new atmosphere. I felt welcome and I felt like I belonged here. These people were like me. They had problems and wanted a new way of life. I was cautious around people, especially men who looked for a relationship with women. I didn't hang out with many people, and I didn't smoke. I did a lot of reading and went to meetings. I had a few good women friends. I started to believe I could stay sober.

I started seeing a guy from Texas. (Strike one.) He was loud, boastful, arrogant, and rude. He was quite fond of himself and on the make. He tried to talk to me, but I wasn't nice to him, and he left me alone. I wasn't nice to anyone, so everybody left me alone. I tried hard to not like this guy, but he was persistent. He thought it was funny that I didn't like him. I thought he reminded me a lot of the guy I just left, and I wasn't about to get into another bad relationship. I was still in a bad marriage. I didn't like this guy and told him so.

This guy realized I wasn't interested in being his girlfriend, so he just started being nice to me. We chatted sometimes, and he asked if I wanted to go to meetings with him. I just couldn't seem to get past his selfishness. Every time we talked, it was always about him. I could hardly get a word in sometimes. I wasn't impressed with him at all. Most people felt the same way.

Finally, we started getting along. I always let know where he stood with me. I talked about my kids a lot. I told him when we started spending more time together that I had kids and would someday have them all together again. I told him that if he wasn't interested in having a family, then he shouldn't pursue me. I knew I wanted my kids back together again. My sobriety and my kids were what I wanted.

The guy invited me to his family's home, and I went with him. We had a good time. There, I saw all the masks that he wore fall away. He was nice, calm, and helpful to his parents. He was thoughtful and respectful, and I started believing that I really liked him.

We spent a lot of time together and eventually moved out of the facility together. We both had sponsors who advised us and who we trusted. They thought we would be okay together as long as we put our sobriety before our relationship. I began to care for him very much.

We moved into an apartment, and I went to find my children. I found my oldest son, and he moved in with us. We followed the same routine that halfway living taught us, but the reality of life started, and we began to fall apart as a couple.

Neither of us had any idea how to live life on life's terms, and we both had baggage from the past and our own selfish ambitions. We fought over money issues, and I learned that he was having affairs. I was insecure and angry that I was in another relationship with someone who cared only for himself and was going to hurt me and disrespect me. We parted ways.

During this time, I felt hurt, humiliated, and disrespected. I didn't know what to do, and I went into depression. I did things on a daily basis, but it was only routine. I went to work and meetings and was always crying to my sponsor. I felt hopeless and defeated again, but this time, I was sober.

I still saw this guy from time to time, and I was always mad at him. We got to where we couldn't be together for five minutes without a blowup. I realized that I was just another conquest for him and decided that guys like him didn't deserve girls like me. I was dating other guys but none seriously. Some of the guys I dated liked me and wanted to be with me, but my heart was stuck on him.

During this time, I worked with my sponsor. I realized I put my faith in a person and not God. I expected him to make me happy, and the only thing he did was make me mad. I had to trust and rely on God if I was ever going to move on with my life. I would never be happy with the way we were getting along. He wasn't able to give me what I needed from a man. He was able to love me as much as he was capable of loving someone, but I wanted more.

We had decided to go to Eureka Springs together for a conference. I took off work. I waited for him to call. When I finally reached someone, they told me he had left without me. He was already there. I was furious. That was it. I had had enough of him not treating me right, and I felt like he left me behind on purpose. He didn't want me to go with him. I was upset. I drove home in tears. I was crying so hard that I had to pull off the highway. I was overcome with hurt over everything. I was done. I hated him. In the moment of hate, I heard a soft voice say, "Stop looking at what he didn't give you, and look at what he did give you." I knew it was the voice of God and got quiet. As I sat on the highway, I realized that he had indeed given me a lot. He introduced me to my sponsor. He encouraged me to work the twelve steps. In that moment, I knew I could live without him, let him go, and not hate him. I made a decision.

I knew this town was not going to be big enough for him and me. I worked for an ice cream store and asked for a transfer. I would go anywhere to get away from him. I came home from a weekend looking for a transfer with new resolve. My friend volunteered to drive my car for me, and I was ready to get a rental truck and start packing. I waited for the transfer to go through. I couldn't stand the thought of seeing him with someone else or running into him somewhere by accident because I loved him, but I was willing to let him go.

When he returned, he was shocked that I was so upset. He didn't see his mistake and thought I was making a big deal out of nothing. I told him of my displeasure and my plans to move to another city. I was willing to walk away and let him go. I was ready to move on. He tried to talk me out of it, but I knew I was done. I let him know that I cared for him but not more that I cared for myself. I tried to make it work to the best of my ability. I could walk away and not look back. I meant that, and he knew it

I didn't know what was going on for him during this time, but I know that he was different, and he was desperate for me not to leave him. He wanted to get back together. He said I could move back in with him. I said no. I told him that living with him didn't work out well for me. I told him that if we lived together, we were going to get married. He froze at the *M* word. I explained that he should know whether he wanted to be with me forever. We had been seeing each other for three years. If there was a doubt, it was okay; he should just let me go. We decided to get back together and start over in a new place. The more we looked for a place, the more I got discouraged. I finally thought, *Maybe we're not supposed to get back together.* Then we found a house. We didn't have to apply for anything. We just made a deposit and moved in. I believed the house was a gift from God.

We still had a lot to learn. I let him know to not hurt me again, and I tried to put to rest things in my past too. We were married in June 2000.

My kids came to live us eight months after we were married, and he helped me raise them. I remember the first time I realized that he was going to help me with the kids who were ten, eleven, and thirteen when they came to live with us. We had just gotten home from a family outing, and my youngest son was mad and started getting ugly on the way home. My daughter was crying, my other son was yelling, and the youngest was cussing. When we got home, my daughter went to her room and slammed the door, my other son went to this room and started throwing things around, and the youngest ran off down the road. I calmed my daughter down, talked with my other son, and set off to find the youngest. He was always getting mad and running off.

I found the youngest and my husband walking back to the house from down the road. I was relieved to realize that he was helping me with these children. I never had help from the men in my life before. I was pleased by this and I loved him more for the help.

Our lives revolved around the sobriety, work, and the kids. My husband was strong and helpful but made mistakes, and I sometimes felt like I had four children living at home, and my husband was the oldest. I finally realized that he was learning to be a father to children who were not his and tried hard to do a good job. I admired his resolve and loved him for it.

As a mother, I was secure in my role and was never

afraid to tell my children the truth or when they were wrong. I also learned to praise my children and encourage them. My role as a wife was harder for me to learn.

I knew I loved my husband, and I knew he loved me too. I was always afraid of other women, and I constantly remembered the past hurt and disrespect. I wondered if he would cheat again and lived in fear that he would! Whenever we went to meetings together, I saw women and young girls who showed my husband a lot of attention that he really liked. I had a problem with that! It took many years for me to realize that women were going to be attracted to him but that I would have to trust my husband. It was only through many painful arguments, and sleepless nights, that I realized the distrust was my own. I carried the memories of the past into today not him. He remained faithful to me even though I didn't believe he had changed from that way of life. He always told me, "Honey, when we got married, I took a vow before God, my family, and our friends, and I meant what I said on that day." We had a long talk over the past and I told him how much the unfaithfulness hurt me even though we weren't married. I told him why I distrusted him and why I kept bringing up the past. We had never talked about it and he finally understood. The distrust was unresolved pain from the past. He apologized to me. I forgave him. God Bless my husband. Finally, we moved past the pain of the past.

Today, my husband is a nice guy. He is handsome. He is always laughing. He smiles a lot, loves to joke and tease, and can laugh at his self. He is dedicated to his sobriety and loves the fellowship of recovery.

Over the years in sobriety, we have grown as a couple and as people. We stay true to our own values and ideals. We are parents to the children who came to us broken, confused, hurt, and abandoned. We are grandparents to their children as well. Our children love us. The children call him before they call me about things. They take him to lunch, and they know he loves them. He came a long way in his fatherhood and looks forward to the day when he will be reunited with his own daughter.

He was reunited with his daughter in 2010. He was very happy to finally be able to see her and talk with her.

One day, I was driving home from work and saw a car on the side of the road. It looked like my son's car, so I called him and asked him if he was stuck on the road and why he didn't call me if he was. He told me that if he was stuck on the side of the road, he would call my husband first! Well, praise the Lord.

I could never say enough nice things about my husband. He is very loving to me. He is patient, kind, gentle, devoted to me and our family, faithful, a hard worker, and determined. He will do anything for me and our family. He has taught me how to be a good wife by being a good husband. He apologizes for his failures and mistakes and never brings up the past. He doesn't yell at me or ever raise his voice to me. He has never hit me. He has never called me anything except my name or sweetheart, and is affectionate to me. If he has any faults, they are that he doesn't know his directions and can't spell. It took many arguments for me to realize this too.

My husband has taken an angry, insecure, frustrated

woman with five children, baggage from the past, and little hope for the future and has helped her to grow into the woman who writes this today. He loved her without fail and loved her children to a level she never knew before. He has saved us all in ways we didn't even know we needed.

My husband calls himself the alpha, but since he doesn't know how to spell, he spells it *alfa*. It is funny, and we hang on to it for him. This is just a story of how God has blessed my life and the lives of my children with my husband. He is everything we needed in a dad and husband, and we will be forever grateful to the Alfa.

9
Learning
to Work

I grew up not knowing that I would have to work someday. I was raised by my grandparents. They owned their home, and my grandpa owned his own pipe straightening company during the oil field boom years. I never had to worry about money, and I wasn't taught the value of money or how to work to earn a living.

During my growing-up days, I thought I was poor. I wasn't given an allowance, and I never had money of my own. I didn't have a job and wasn't encouraged to get one. I didn't have a car or the things that kids have as they grow up. My grandma was a housewife, and her hobby was sewing. I always felt poor because I never had any money. I learned not to value money because I never had it or knew the value of money.

In the tenth grade, I got a job selling coupon books over the phone. I used to walk to work. I worked a block from my house. I had to quit my job after a week because I had to go out of town with my grandparents.

When I was eighteen, I had my first son. I lived with an aunt, and she helped me get a job at Montgomery Ward, where she worked. When I got paid by the store, I used to give my aunt half of my check. I got paid $3.55 an hour. I worked part-time. That was a lot of money for me, and my aunt helped me spend it on things for my son, like diapers and clothes.

During my lifetime, I had lots of jobs. I have worked as a waitress. I cleaned motel rooms. I worked in stores, and I was a telemarketer. I never kept a job long. I always had a man to take care of me. I didn't realize until I was in my thirties that I had no work ethic. I didn't care if I had any money. I barely knew how to pay bills when I got married. I never knew how to spend money when I did have a job.

In 1992, I got a good job in a warehouse. I used to fill invoice orders for stores with general merchandise. My department was hair care products. I worked Monday through Friday from 7:00 a.m. to 3:30 p.m. It was a good job, and I was good at it. I made good money. I served on the standards committee and was successful in my job for the first time in my life. I had this job for more than three years. I used my money to help with the bills and meet the needs of my children. I quit this job due to a drug habit.

In 1996, I moved to a new city. My first job was at Sam's. I made pizza. It was only a seasonal job. I was let go after the first of the year. I had that job for two months. I was disappointed.

I was thirty-two years old. I had to learn to work and earn a living by myself. I was in recovery and had a sponsor. I was learning to live life on life's terms. I didn't like the idea of having to work. I was learning to be self-sufficient. It was a hard lesson to learn.

After I was let go from Sam's, I got another job at an ice cream store during the morning shift. I lived in a halfway house for women, so I rode the bus to work. I had to learn to do that too. I worked from 7:00 a.m. to 3:30 p.m. I did a good job. I was fast and picked up things quickly. The morning shift manager liked my hard work, and we became friends. I asked her if I could work on her shift, and she said yes, but her shift started at 5:00 a.m. She asked me if I could get a ride to work. I told her no. She moved me to her shift and said she would pick me up every morning. I didn't like this job, but it paid me money. I didn't have an education or many choices.

One day, my manager told me she had to go by her house before she took me home, and I realized that she lived around the corner from the store. She went out of her way every day to pick me up and drop me off. I was moved in my heart and realized that I was a good worker. This made me feel good, and I tried even harder. In three months, I became the morning shift manager, and my boss became the morning assistant manager. We both got promoted. By now, I had a boyfriend. We were living together, and I drove his car.

During this time, I learned to be faithful to my job. I learned this from my boyfriend, who later became my husband. He always went to work. He never missed. If he was sick or stayed up late, he still went to work. I couldn't let him be better at something than I was. I went to work every day too. In about a year, my boss moved to another store, and I became the morning assistant manager. I made ten dollars an hour, and I was happy about that. I walked out on this job after I got mad at my store manager for not standing behind a decision that I made concerning an angry employee.

I got a job working at a bingo hall. I didn't know about bingo or the drama that would unfold there. Bingo is a world of its own, and you better know what you're doing in there, or they will eat you alive. I was hired as a food server. I took orders for those who played bingo. The man who owned the bingo hall noticed that I moved fast and talked to everyone. I was hired as a floor runner. I sold bingo sheets and took money. Once I figured out what I was doing and the object of the game, I did well there. I made a lot of money in tips, which my coworkers did not like at all. The runners sat after closing and counted their tips together, but not me. I did not want them to know the amount of tips I got a night. I was the outsider. I didn't care.

At the bingo hall, I realized I loved the money too much. I hit several people. I started to behave badly. I knew it was time to go when I started getting the crappy job of selling tickets or something that didn't pay in tips. I got no tips doing this, and I didn't get along with the other runners. One of them was sweet on the boss's daughter, who also worked there. I walked out on that job too.

I ended up going back to the ice cream store. I was

grateful they hired me back. I didn't like it, and I was there about a year before I was let go there too. I was angry that I was let go. At this time, I was going through a custody battle for my children, and I needed time off on a weekend. I wasn't given the weekend off to be with my kids, so I took it off. When I returned to work on Monday, I was already replaced.

I worked a few temporary jobs for about nine months. I worked as an order filler. I worked in an electronic store, putting out stock, and I worked for a printing company. I also worked for one day at a leading plastic company. I came home in tears and begged my husband to not make me go back. It was the most horrible place I worked in my life, and I told them so when I picked up my check.

In 2001, the nation was still reeling from September 11. During a Thanksgiving gathering in Dallas with my husband's family one of the old guys there asked me where I was working. I was at the printing company. He told me to go to the airport and get one of those security jobs. He said they were going to be federal someday. I didn't know what that meant, but when I got back home, I went to the airport and filled out an application. They were nice and said they would get back to me. I waited a day with no word, so I called them. Dale, the boss, said he hadn't looked at my application yet but that he would. I waited another day. I called back. I did this every day. He would tell me he needed something, and I would get it to him. I would call him again. I called him every day for a week. Finally, Dale said, "Can you come in tomorrow to pick up your uniform?"

I said, "I can come in today!"

He said, "No, come in tomorrow." When I went to get my uniform, he told me he hired me just so I would stop calling him. This was the first time I persisted to get a job. It paid off.

I worked at security. I went through a week of training. I was taught to use the basic security tools. I was put with a woman who shadowed me for several weeks, and I learned quickly. I passed all my tests. I enjoyed this work, and I strived to be the best I could be. I made friends quickly and felt my job was important. I was in the last class hired by the airport after September 11. I worked for this company for almost a year. In the fall of 2002, the federal government came in to take over all the security.

A lot of rumors went around about the private security workers not being able to cross over into the federal jobs. I wondered if I would have a job at all. I learned there was a background check and police record check, and my heart sank. I had a history of arrests and jail time during my drinking days. I talked with my boss, Dale, about this, and he asked what kind of trouble I got into. I told him, and he smiled and encouraged me. He said those weren't the kinds of things they were looking at but to be honest about them on my application. I was stressed and worried. I had never applied for a federal job. The application was online, and computers are my enemy, so I had a difficult time, but I completed the application and sent it off. I hoped and prayed.

Sometime later, I was at work, and a call came. Four of us had interviews the next morning. We were to be at the testing site by 6:00 a.m. It was 6:00 p.m. then. We knew we had a whole day of testing ahead, and arrangements were made to get to the city, spend the night, and be ready the next day. Everything worked out except the ready part.

The next day was confusing and stressful. There must have been a hundred people there. We were told to sit and wait. "Go to this room." Then we talked to someone and either moved to the next room or were asked to leave. I kept moving to the next room. There were reading tests, image tests, color tests, eye tests, hearing tests, and lifting tests. I talked to many people. I kept moving and praying. I got scared; at some point, all the people I started with weren't there anymore.

I moved to a room to go over my application. I thought, *Now, I'll be asked to leave.* I kept moving. At the final stage, I was asked, "Why do you want to work for Homeland Security?"

I said, "To protect the homeland." I meant that. My eyes teared up. I remembered the towers falling, the pain on people's faces, and the uncertainty of September 11. The tests were done, and I was told I was an acceptable candidate. I was accepted for a temporary position of five years. I accepted and filled out mounds of papers. The day was finished, and it was 6:00 p.m. The twelve hours were long and grueling, but I felt happy to be a part of Homeland Security.

Weeks later, I was sent to another training site for a week of classroom training. Then I went home to weeks of on-the-job training.

As of this writing, I have been with Homeland Security

for ten years. I have been at the airport for eleven years. I love my job. I worked security for six years and have spent the last four years working as an additional layer of security. I love this job as well.

My job history since I got in recovery astounds me. I had never been at any job long. I know I am growing up as well as growing older. I am thankful for my job, and I feel I provide a service to the people of America. I care about the job I do, and I do it willingly and with pride. I feel honored that God has blessed me with a good job and a work ethic that I know that He gave me. He put people in my life who taught me the value of going to work every day and doing a good job while I'm there. I appreciate that. I'm allowed to wear a uniform that I feel privileged to wear, and I get to be a servant to the people who travel.

Not bad for a little Indian girl who came into recovery Broke, broken, no work ethic and no idea how to live sober. Praise the Lord!

Epilogue

As I write this closing, I still praise God for His complete faithfulness to my family. It is only by His grace and mercy that I have a story to share. As I look back over the years, I see His divine hand over my life. I live today to share that story with you.

B and his wife have just had their third child, another son. It was a complete surprise to my son that his wife was pregnant, and he has faced a lot of fears. In the end, he is happy and is still a good father to his sons. He continues to have a relationship with his daddy and siblings from his daddy's side of the family.

Gabriel is making a move to be with the family. He is divorced from his children's mother but gets to see his sons regularly. During the holiday visit, he let me know that he felt he wasn't as strong as the rest of the kids because I gave him up for adoption. I assured him he has the same blood and is indeed just as strong as the rest of the family. He is just getting a late start. I assured him that *all* of us started at the same place he is at. He will begin his journey getting to know us on an everyday level, and we look forward to helping him and encouraging him to be all that God has in store for him.

My daughter, Krissy, is currently living in Georgia and isn't speaking to me. I had to make some hard decisions concerning her and her daughter. It was hard to do. As a result of that decision, my daughter has removed herself from the family and is walking her own road to adulthood. I pray for her and for God's will in her life. I love her and I miss her deeply. She is my only daughter. I trust God. I am currently writing the story of Krissy.

Bug still works at United Airlines. He lives close to me and has been with his girlfriend for several years. He recently started dancing with us in powwows. He is still leading others with his example of complete integrity at home and at work. He has received several awards for his work ethic and skills from United Airlines. His younger brother, Jodie, told me that it was Bug's work ethic that helped Jodie gain his own work ethic. His eyes welled up as he told how much Bug helped to save him from his old way of life. Bug has always been a great example of courage, dignity, and strong family values.

Jodie and his wife are expecting their first child in August 2013. They have walked a long, hard road together. Jodie told me that being married has helped him grow up and think of others. He is working and doing well. When I read Jodie this story for the book, his wife was there too. When I came to the part about Jodie becoming a preacher, she told me that she always wanted to be the wife of a preacher. See how God works? I smiled and thanked God for His mercy and grace.

The Alfa is doing well. He bought a tool franchise and works constantly. We enjoy dancing in powwows around the state. He is still devoted to our marriage, our family, and sobriety.

I am still at Homeland Security. I enjoy dancing in powwows and spending time with my children and grandchildren. I praise the Lord for all the additions to our family and tell the kids to "bring on the babies." They laugh and ask me if I took my medicine for the day.

This year, my oldest son will be thirty years old. I can't seem to wrap my brain around that.

I still attend my church. I love my church family.

Thank you for reading this book. I hope it will inspire you to keep walking with and trusting God.

CPSIA information can be obtained at www.ICGtesting.com
Printed in the USA
LVOW13s2233100913

351913LV00001B/14/P